PARACHUTES FOR SHEEP

J. CHRISTOPHER MCMICHAEL

Parachutes for Sheep
Copyright © 2020 by J. Christopher McMichael

Published by Engrafted Word Church
5 W. Broad Street, Cookeville, TN 38501
www.EngraftedWord.org

All rights reserved. No part of this book may be reproduced or transmitted in any form or by any means without written permission from the author.

ISBN: 978-1-7339629-2-6

Unless otherwise indicated, all Scripture quotations are from the King James Version of the Bible.

Scripture quotations labeled NASB are from the New American Standard Bible® (NASB), Copyright © 1960, 1962, 1963, 1968, 1971, 1972, 1973, 1975, 1977, 1995 by The Lockman Foundation. Used by permission.

Scripture quotations designated NET are from the NET Bible® copyright ©1996, 2019 by Biblical Studies Press, L.L.C. http://netbible.com. All rights reserved.

Scripture quotations marked CSB have been taken from the Christian Standard Bible®, Copyright © 2017 by Holman Bible Publishers. Used by permission. Christian Standard Bible® and CSB® are federally registered trademarks of Holman Bible Publishers.

Scripture quotations marked NLT are taken from the Holy Bible, New Living Translation, copyright ©1996, 2004, 2015 by Tyndale House Foundation. Used by permission of Tyndale House Publishers, Inc., Carol Stream, Illinois 60188. All rights reserved.

Cover layout by Darrell Kerley
Cover Art by Marlin Peterson

Printed in the United States of America

To God's pastors, the principals of His flock.

CONTENTS

Introduction 1

Part One: The Church, The Pastor, and You!

Chapter 1 9
The History of the Church and The Office of Pastor

Chapter 2 21
Biblical Shepherding

Chapter 3 28
God Picks Your Church

Chapter 4 44
Root Ball Christians

Chapter 5 52
General Dos and Don'ts (When Leaving a Church)

Part Two: The Six Parachutes of Church Departure

Chapter 6 67
The "Divine Reassignment" Parachute

Chapter 7 76
The "Fleeing Apostasy" Parachute

Chapter 8 86
The "I'm Hungrier for More of God" Parachute

Chapter 9 93
The "Geographical Move" Parachute

Chapter 10 102
The "Search For an Easier Church" Parachute

Chapter 11 111
The "I'm Offended" Parachute

Chapter 12 120
Conclusion

INTRODUCTION

As a pastor, I have been blessed to be surrounded by many men and women much more experienced in the faith than me. After my wife and I had our first child, I received a round of invaluable advice and wisdom from many senior pastors and ministers. There was no shortage of parenting input here and tidbits of caution there, but one word of admonition still sticks out to me more than any other, and I believe it is apropos to the subject of this book. The warning went something like this:

> *Pastor Chris, you make sure you enjoy that baby and protect her. You enjoy that wife and protect her, too. Don't ever neglect them for the ministry or that congregation. You need to know and understand that at any given minute half of that church of yours could up and abandon you without so much as saying "goodbye" or even "thank you" for all you ever did for them. But your wife and daughter will always be there. Those sheep are replaceable, but your family is not.*

Prior to this bit of wisdom, my wife and I had experienced the occasional disappointment and pain of having a family or individual leave our church, but the extreme image my friend painted for me put pastoring in a different perspective. I think it may have been his use of the word "abandon" that changed how I viewed what I shall call "the act of carnal church departure." But can you imagine that? What some Christians call "changing churches" might more accurately be called *abandonment* or *betrayal*. The purpose of this book is to help prevent any such future carnal exits. I do *not* aim to prevent church departures—I seek to prevent *carnal* church departures.

Nothing hurts a real pastor like watching a precious family leave their church the wrong way, and I don't believe I know a single pastor who has not been hurt by the separation of a family they had so deeply invested in. Though I understand people will come and go, believers must still be taught the proper way to do so.

It wasn't all that long ago in Western Culture that a Christian was dedicated as a baby, married, and eulogized—all in the same church, at the same altar, sometimes even by the same pastor. If you ever get to visit an old country church, you may be able to find a cemetery on the church property (usually adjacent to the church), filled with only a handful of last names because, traditionally, people spent their entire life at the same church, marrying within the church, and raising generation after generation in the same place. I make this cultural observation, not to necessarily promote it, but to simply point out how much Western Church culture has changed in the last few generations.

Today, people rarely (if ever) live and die in the same town, much less the same church. Most modern believers have a church attendance list that looks more like a job resumé—2 years at this church, 6 months at that church, 1 year of no church, 4.5 years as a deacon here, etc. Needless to say, mobility is on the rise, and Christians are changing churches like never before. My first pastor observed the beginnings of this phenomenon in the mid-1990s as established believers left their old churches and began the new practice of church hopping. He sarcastically called it "the ministry of the traveling Christian." He also lamented, "We're no longer seeing true church growth. This is just church shifting."

INTRODUCTION

From my observations, there are six reasons for this change in Christian behavior. Three of these are sound, reasonable, and perhaps inevitable. The other three tread upon diabolical and dangerous ground. I will briefly present each of them here and then explore each one in more detail in the following chapters. As the title of the book implies, we will prescribe a parachute of Bible-based wisdom for each scenario. The merits of each reason for changing churches will be evaluated for the believers who find themselves in such a situation, so they may safely land at their new church.

The first and most biblical reason Christians are leaving churches is because of **divine reassignment**. This reason is both the rarest and yet best to leave one church for another. These believers are either being sent out by their existing pastor to help start a work or to go and serve at another solid church where the will of God has retasked them to help. This is the ideal condition for leaving a church because regardless of where they land, the believer is still serving God. God will never authorize a Christian to leave one church to go and do nothing at another church. This subject will be covered in Chapter 6 more thoroughly.

Second, as humanity winds down and the Lord's return approaches, many preachers, churches, and even whole denominations are self-corrupting and defecting from the way of truth. These groups are fulfilling the many prophecies about the apostasy of the last days. As a result, many Christians, in their fidelity to the Holy Scriptures and allegiance to Christ, are exiting their congregations in search of wholesome doctrine and true pastors. These precious believers reject hirelings, perverted ministers, poisonous weeds, and muddy water; they simply want a righteous shepherd, green grass, and still waters. Chapter 7 will evaluate how to leave an **apostate** or **corrupt church** in order to stay faithful to Jesus Christ.

Chapter 8 will look at the third biblical reason for the surge in transient Christianity—**divine hunger**. Some Christians find themselves hungrier for more than what their current church is offering. Whether it be hunger for better teaching, the presence of the Holy Spirit, more evangelism, or simply a church that is more alive than dead, saints are leaving lukewarm or mediocre churches for something teeming with the presence of God.

Spiritual hunger is a powerful motivator for changing churches, and hungry Christians will make great sacrifices to find the presence of God. As one Christian explained when asked why he chose to attend a church so far from his house, "It's worth the drive if the church is alive."

Chapter 9 will look at the fourth reason for so much church shifting—the **geographical move**. Just as most Americans no longer live and die in the same city anymore, very few Christians will live and die in the same church. Young people grow up and leave the town or city of their childhood, and in doing so, change churches. Some believers are being relocated by their boss or their own career endeavors. Still, some move to be closer to family. Others leave to pursue the American Dream (funny how that never seems to include God). These believers are leaving their church because of a geographical move. This motive is *not* necessarily a biblical reason to change churches. This is the first of our six motives that becomes questionable, and every Christian must be very cautious in these scenarios.

The fifth, and most rebellious, reason for so much interchurch movement, is that modern Christians aren't as strong and mature as the saints of yesteryear. In fulfillment of another end-times prophecy, generally speaking, many Christians can no longer endure sound doctrine, "but after their own lusts shall they heap to themselves teachers, having itching ears; and they shall turn away their ears from the truth, and shall be turned unto fables."[1] Simply put, these believers are leaving solid Bible churches in search of an **easier option**. This is an incredibly deceitful motive. It will be discussed more in Chapter 10.

The sixth and final reason we will evaluate in this book is **offense**. Some people change churches simply because they have been offended by the pastor, a leader, some church practice, or someone in the church. This makes the church look more like a grade school playground rather than the army of the Living God. We will discuss the subject of offense and what can be done about it in Chapter 11.

I suppose we could tack on a seventh reason to leave church—**quitting God**! This is becoming very common, too. In such a situation, there is no

---

[1] See 2 Timothy 4:3-4.

INTRODUCTION

safe or honorable way to depart because such a departure will have no safe landing. Such a believer isn't just quitting church; they are departing the faith. This is never wise, nor does it ever produce an improvement in life. Quitting church is tantamount to pruning oneself off the Vine. It's spiritual suicide. Don't do this!

There is a right way to leave a church and there is a wrong way to leave a church.

The wrong way comes naturally for the sin nature. The right way, well unfortunately, the right way to leave a church probably hasn't been taught like it should have been. Pastors are so eager to get believers to join their congregations, it seems as though good teaching on exit protocols has either been overlooked or neglected. Or maybe it's just the joyful naïveté of a good-natured pastor failing to consider that not every current church member will finish their race at his church.

It is a fact of Kingdom life: people will always come and go from the local church. The late Dr. George Evans coined one of the greatest of all pastoral proverbs:

"Pastoring is like driving a bus. People get on. People get off. Pastors . . . just drive the bus."

Leaving the local church must be done honorably! To leave dishonorably is so dangerous. It is my prayer that this book can provide some biblical insights into how a Christian can honorably and properly leave their church. It is my hope that pastors will pick up this book and further propagate some of the honorable truths contained herein.

Although the purpose of this book is to teach some general rules and procedures on how to honorably change churches, the first part of the book establishes doctrinal context. The first three chapters cover a brief history of the Church, the role and job description of the local pastor, the importance of church attendance, how to find the church God has assigned you to, and finally, how to put down roots and be faithful.

In Chapter 4 we will evaluate the allegory of root ball Christianity and how that relates to being faithful to the church God has assigned you to.

Chapter 5 will focus on the importance of an honorable church departure and evaluate the results of a simple pastoral poll I undertook for this book. It will also look at several basic dos and don'ts when it comes to church departure.

The second part of the book, beginning with Chapter 6, will discuss how to properly leave a church in each of the given scenarios.

I have not written this book with the megachurch in mind but for the average American church, which even at the time of this writing (2020) only has about 80 members. That is not to say that larger churches and their members won't benefit from the truths contained herein, but megachurches have so much foot traffic that it's easy to come and go without anyone ever knowing you, much less miss you when you never come back. Though carnal departures can hurt big churches, it is the smaller church—the 25- to 250-member church—that suffers the most when a family, or even just an individual, leaves dishonorably. So read on to learn how to honor God when you change churches as you discover *Parachutes for Sheep*!

J. Christopher McMichael
June 2020

PART ONE

The Church, The Pastor, And You!

1

THE HISTORY OF THE CHURCH AND THE OFFICE OF PASTOR

Though the aim of this book is to teach Christians how to honorably exit a local church, we would be remiss if we did not take a moment and briefly cover the essence and nature of the local church and its leader—the local pastor. It is necessary for every Christian to know what God has called them to be a part of (the local church) and to understand the role and assignment of its leader (the local pastor) in order to appreciate why leaving a local church should not be taken lightly.

The Church is, without a doubt, the Lord's crown jewel. The Lord Jesus Christ has been building His Church ever since His ascension. Every Christian is called to a local church, and no Christian will ever finish their divine race or fulfill their destiny without the necessary influence of the local church.

God has designed the church to be a refuge for the believer. It's like a supernatural docking station where believers can be recharged and receive supernatural downloads. It is where the believers are protected, matured, equipped, and even dispatched into ministry. The local church is where we are trained and given a place to serve. It's where we meet our spouses, marry them, dedicate our babies, and raise them in the fear and admonition of the Lord.

The local church is also meant to be the headwaters of all *Great Commission* activities (preaching the Gospel and making disciples). It is the forward operating base from where all soul-winning and discipleship takes place. The local congregation expands the Kingdom of God through evangelism and discipleship. These new disciples in turn reach their friends, win them to Christ, and bring them to the House of God for further discipleship. This is how the Kingdom expands. It follows the pattern of sheep begetting more sheep.

Contrary to modern ideologies and marketing strategies, we don't get to pick and choose where we go to church. The Lord sets every believer in His Body as it pleases Him.[1] According to the Old Testament pattern, God calls His name in a unique place for every family.[2] In ancient times, the whole of Israel did not go up to Jerusalem to worship every Sabbath. This would have been logistically impossible. The Tabernacle at Shiloh (and later the Temple at Jerusalem) were only visited once a year on the Day of Atonement. Instead, localized individual altars were erected all over Israel where God had called His name for His people.

After they were taken away as slaves into Babylon, the Jews developed the synagogue system, complete with a local ruler, or overseer.[3,4,5] As a displaced people, geographically far-removed from their destroyed Temple, the Jews still required a place to assemble, worship, and receive instruction from the Torah. Thus, the synagogue system developed out of necessity. While sacrifice was the focal point of Solomon's Temple, instruction and teaching were the emphases of the synagogues. The synagogue system was established so that every Israelite could hear the Law of

---

[1] 1 Corinthians 12:18
[2] See Exodus 20:24 and Deuteronomy 12:5-7.
[3] The Zondervan Pictorial Bible Dictionary, 1967, Zondervan Publishing House, p. 817-819, *Synagogue* entry.
[4] Halley's Bible Handbook with the New International Version: Completely revised and expanded 25th edition of Halley's Bible Handbook, Zondervan, Grand Rapids, MI 2007, p. 487-488, *Synagogue* entry.
[5] The Jewish Encyclopedia, 1906, *Synagogue* entry.

Moses every Sabbath, not just once every seven years as was the case before the Exile.[6]

After the completion of Zerubbabel's Temple, the subsequent revival of Ezra and Nehemiah's day saw the reinstitution of the Temple system complete with all its sacrifices. At this time Ezra also imported the synagogue system from captivity. For the next 400 years, until the Resurrection of Jesus Christ and the advent of the Church Age, both the Temple system and the synagogue system ran simultaneously. If you will recall, Jesus preached in both the Temple *and* the synagogues during His earthly ministry.

History and theology show that the early church adopted its pattern for church service (that is assembly, worship, and instruction) from the synagogue system. And why not? As the old adage says, "if it ain't broke, don't fix it." The transition from Old Testament worship to New Testament Church was not instantaneous. In the early days following the Resurrection of Jesus Christ, the first Christians were considered a sect of Judaism—one that followed "the Way." They saw no reason to reject the Law of Moses, Jewish traditions, or the authority of the Temple. They did, however, add two new rites: believer's water baptism and communion.

The early believers were still learning how to walk out "the new and living way," so they retained a lot of Jewish customs for years to come. A close analysis of the Book of Acts easily reveals that the early Church met in homes for private prayer,[7] but also continued to worship at the Temple[8] and in synagogues.[9]

As the apostles spread out all over Asia Minor, they continued the Jewish tradition of teaching in the synagogues on the Sabbath. They even continued teaching from Moses and the Prophets; the only change made was to the message they delivered—Christ crucified.[10] This pattern of

---

[6] Deuteronomy 31:9-13
[7] See Acts 1:13, 2:1; 4:23-31; 12:12-19.
[8] See Acts 3:1-3; 21:22-30; 22:17-18.
[9] The word "assembly" in James 2:2, implying "church assembly," is the Greek word *synagoge*.
[10] See Acts 13:14-43; 14:1; 17:1-4, 10-12, 16-17; 18:4, 19, 26.

Sabbath-day synagogue reasoning is even called "Paul's custom" in Acts 17:2 (NASB).

The church at Jerusalem remained very strict and, in many ways, legalistic. Meanwhile the Hellenized[11] churches outside of Jerusalem and throughout the Roman Empire were free from Jewish tradition and grew more in line with what we now recognize as New Testament doctrine.

The Christians at Jerusalem continued to be counted as a sect of Judaism until the Jews revolted against the Roman Empire in 66 A.D. When this fatal revolt began, the leaders of the Jerusalem church were warned in a vision to flee the city. The Jewish revolt was ultimately put down, and the Temple was utterly destroyed in 70 A.D. Famed Church Historian Bruce L. Shelley succinctly describes the events as follows:

Pious Jews considered the Christian flight an act of treason, and it sealed the fate of the church in the Jewish world. With the decision to bar Christian Jews from synagogue services some years later, the break was complete. Any Jew who wished to remain faithful to his religion could not also be a Christian. The new faith had become and would remain a gentile movement. The old wineskin was irreparably torn.[12]

As the Lord used the Apostles to progressively reveal proper New Testament doctrine, the early Church slowly moved away from many Jewish customs and grew into the universal body of Christ we know today. The most common form of church governments was set forth by Ignatius (the pastor) of Antioch. Based on his interpretation of the Apostles' epistles, he wrote a series of letters around the end of the first century.[13]

---

[11] Greek in character. When applied to Jews or early Christians, it refers to those who were born outside of Israel, spoke Greek, and were Greek, not Jewish, in their culture.

[12] Shelley, Bruce L. 2013. *Church History in Plain Language.* 4th ed. Nashville, Tennessee: Thomas Nelson, p. 24.

[13] It must be noted that Ignatius of Antioch's letters are not Canon and therefore cannot be taken as Scripture. They are considered part of the Early Church Fathers' writings.

In them, he set forth the pattern of a singular bishop (or pastor) over each church, then a body of presbyters, and finally, a company of deacons. He taught, "God's grace and the Spirit's power, flow to flock through this united ministry."[14] This general pattern rapidly spread throughout Christendom and is still widely followed in the present day.

Today, as in the days of the synagogue system, believers can't all worship in the same assembly or at the same location. According to New Testament doctrine, every Christian is, paradoxically, the Temple of the Holy Spirit but still assigned to a local church led by a local pastor.

The Local Pastor

The words *pastor* and *shepherd* are synonymous. Both terms describe a man responsible for the care of a flock of sheep. In His wisdom, God chose this allegory to describe the nature of the relationship between the leader and his flock. According to the sheep/shepherd relationship, the local pastor is the only minister of the Gospel responsible for a flock. Evangelists evangelize, teachers teach, prophets prophesy, but pastors live for the local flock.[15]

Pastors are the most prolific of all Gospel ministers. They preach more sermons, marry more couples, dedicate more babies, mend more marriages, train more leaders, and bury more saints than any other kind of minister in the Body of Christ. The prophet Jeremiah called pastors "the principal of the flock."[16] They are the overseers and superintendents of the local church with all of its programs, buildings, discipleship classes, outreaches, missionary projects, and community influence. Shepherds

---

[14] Ibid., pg. 76.
[15] It should be observed that apostles can do all of the above. This is part of their gifting in church planting. The main difference between a pastor and an apostle would be that a pure pastor will be assigned to his flock for a long time while the apostle will start a church, appoint a pastor, then move on. The practice of rotating their pastors every few years by some denominations, while well-intentioned, is not biblically founded.
[16] See Jeremiah 25:34-36. The Hebrew means *great one, majestic one, nobleman, chieftain, prince,* and *leader.*

walk with their sheep through every season of life—good and bad. A good shepherd knows your name. A great shepherd smells like his sheep.

The Greek New Testament word for pastor is *poimen*. This word is used 18 times in the New Testament but is usually translated "shepherd." The Bible describes Jesus as a *poimen* (shepherd) six times. *Poimen* is translated as "shepherd" allegorically eight times and literally four times, but strangely, only once in reference to "pastor," the most important New Testament officer.[17] Just once!

The observant Christian should ask: if the local pastor is so important to the success of a church, why is so little mentioned of him in the New Testament? Good question. The answer: the office or position of pastor/shepherd was thoroughly established in the Old Testament. There is therefore no reason to rehash it in the New Testament. In fact, the pastor is the most established leader in the entire Old Testament. And remember, the New Testament is built upon the established foundation of the Old Testament.[18]

When we refer to Old Testament leaders, we must exclude the office of priest and the priesthood because their job was to minister to the Lord,[19] not lead God's people. It must also be understood that all of God's executive leaders (e.g., judges, kings, and prophets) were all referred to as shepherds in Scripture. This implies that God views His executive leaders as shepherds.

The Hebrew word for shepherd is *ra'ah*. It is used 173 times in the Old Testament and employs a wide use of husbandry[20] and agricultural

---

[17] Jesus as *poimen*: John 10:11, 14, 16; Hebrews 13:20; 1 Peter 2:25. *Poimen* used literally: Luke 2:8, 15, 18, 20. *Poimen* used allegorically: Matthew 9:36; 25:32; 26:31; Mark 6:34; 14:27; John 10:2, 12, 16. *Poimen* used as the overseer of a local church congregation: Ephesians 4:11.

[18] There are many concepts that are thoroughly established in the Old Testament that are not heavily rehashed in the New Testament such as praise, worship, tithing, church governments, etc.

[19] See Exodus 28:3-4, 41; 29:1, 44; 30:30; 40:13, 15; Leviticus 7:35; Deuteronomy 17:12.

[20] The cultivation and production of crops or animals for food.

definitions such as *to feed a flock, to pasture,*[21] *to tend, to nourish*, and figuratively *to guard, to care for, to rule, to govern*. To that end, the term shepherd (*ra'ah*) refers to God's executive leaders 48 times. In fact, when translating *ra'ah,* many of the modern Bible translations use the word "ruler" or "leader" in place of shepherd/pastor.

The Old Testament Job Description

Moses was Israel's first pastor,[22] followed by Joshua,[23] then the judges.[24] The kings were all considered pastors and, without a doubt, David was by far their best shepherd.[25] Shockingly, wicked King Ahab was considered a pastor.[26] Equally surprising, the Lord said of the Persian king Cyrus, "He is my shepherd."[27] Even Jeremiah the prophet was called a pastor, revealing that though not every prophet was a pastor, it is certainly evident some prophets did a lot more than just prophesy and rebuke.[28]

Based on all of the available scriptures concerning shepherds and their flocks, we can easily develop a biblical job description for pastors. The following list is taken directly from the lives and testimonies of Israel's executive leaders. Here is a list of 12 job descriptors that God expected from an Old Testament pastor:

1. Follow God wholeheartedly (Jeremiah 17:16).
2. Have the Holy Spirit (Isaiah 63:11-12a).
3. Be set *over* the congregation, not equal to it (Numbers 27:15-17).
4. Lead God's people through difficult times (Psalm 78:52).
5. Deliver God's people from their enemies (Exodus 2:19).
6. Judge God's people (Judges 3:9-11).

---

[21] To feed livestock by putting them out to graze.
[22] See Psalm 78:52 and Isaiah 63:11-12a.
[23] Numbers 27:15-18
[24] 1 Chronicles 17:6
[25] See 2 Samuel 5:2, 7:7; 1 Chronicles 11:2, 17:6; Psalm 78:71-72.
[26] See 1 Kings 22:17 and 2 Chronicles 18:16.
[27] Isaiah 44:28
[28] Jeremiah 17:16

7. Lead God's people in battle (Judges 3:9-11).
8. Provide rest for God's people (Judges 3:9-11).
9. Refresh God's people with pure water (Exodus 2:19, 15:23-25, 17:4-6; Numbers 20:10-11).
10. Go out before and come in before God's people (2 Samuel 5:2; 1 Chronicles 11:2).
11. Command the officers, not vice-versa (Joshua 1:9-10).
12. Feed God's people (1 Chronicles 17:6; Psalm 78:71-72; Jeremiah 3:15, 23:4; Ezekiel 34:2).

It would be appropriate for believers today to study this list of qualities and expect to find them in New Testament pastors. Granted, a few descriptors may need to be principalized before being applied, for example:

- **Item 7**—Pastors now lead in spiritual battles, not physical warfare.
- **Item 9**—Pastors don't literally provide pure H_2O, but they do wash with the water of the Word.
- **Item 12**—Pastors might call for a church fellowship dinner, but their real New Testament job is to feed God's people the Word.

Dirty Shepherds

The greatest density of *ra'ah* as a local spiritual leader (i.e., the pastor) occurs in the books of Jeremiah and Ezekiel (24 times!). However, a review of these passages reveals many warnings and rebukes. Both of these prophets repeatedly prophesied against the defiled, disgraced, and selfish pastors of Israel. The pastors were leading Israel astray, and God was angry.

Jeremiah prophesied from Palestine in approximately 650 B.C. God called him to warn Judah of the impending divine judgment for their unrepentant idolatry and wickedness. In one sense, he was the last demonstration of God's mercy before Babylonian captivity. Sadly, he was not successful in turning Judah away from sin. Jeremiah lived to see the horrible defeat of Judah by the hand of the Babylonian king, Nebuchadnezzar.

Ezekiel, on the other hand, prophesied as an exile in Persia around the year 620 B.C. His prophecies and judgments continued to address not just the unrepentant Israelites, but more specifically their spiritual leaders.

It is clear from both Jeremiah's and Ezekiel's prophecies that God held and continues to hold pastors responsible for the spiritual health and strength of His people and their nation. As goes the shepherd, so goes the flock. As go the flocks, so goes the nation. The rebukes pronounced against Israel's corrupt shepherds provide further insight into the office and responsibility of biblical pastors. Consider the following rebuke (emphasis mine):

> **The priests said not, Where is the LORD? and they that handle the law knew me not: <u>the pastors also transgressed against me</u>, and the prophets prophesied by Baal, and walked after things that do not profit.**   **Jeremiah 2:8**

This beginning of many prophetic rebukes against Judah's spiritual leadership addresses four categories of leaders:

1. **Priests**—They didn't seek God.
2. **Lawyers** (or scribes) "they that handle the law"—They didn't even know God.
3. **Pastors**—They sinned against God.
4. **Prophets**—They prophesied by demons and sought vanity.

During the judgment of Jeremiah's day, God held each of these four groups of ministers responsible for the condition of the sheep. Israel could only stray from God if their leaders had done so first. Even though every category of spiritual leader had grown corrupt, special blame was reserved for the pastors. Consider the following verses from Jeremiah (all emphases are mine):

> <u>The pastors have become brutish (stupid)</u>, and have not sought the LORD: therefore they shall not prosper, and all their flocks shall be scattered. Jeremiah 10:21

> <u>Many pastors have destroyed my vineyard</u>, they have trodden my portion under foot, they have made my pleasant portion a desolate wilderness. Jeremiah 12:10

> <u>Woe unto the pastors</u> that destroy and scatter the sheep of my pasture! saith the LORD. Jeremiah 23:1

> Therefore thus saith the LORD God of Israel <u>against the pastors</u> that feed my people; Ye have scattered my flock, and driven them away, and have not visited them: behold I will visit upon you the evil of your doings, saith the LORD. Jeremiah 23:2

> My people hath been lost sheep: <u>their shepherds have caused them to go astray</u>, they have turned them away on the mountains: they have gone from mountain to hill, they have forgotten their restingplace. Jeremiah 50:6

Ezekiel prophesied similar things against Israel's pastors:

> Son of man, <u>prophesy against the shepherds (pastors)</u> of Israel, prophesy, and say unto them, Thus saith the Lord GOD unto the shepherds; Woe be to the shepherds of Israel that do feed themselves! Should not the shepherds feed the flocks? Ezekiel 34:2

> As surely as I live, says the Sovereign LORD, you abandoned my flock and left them to be attacked by every wild animal. And <u>though you were my shepherds</u>, you didn't search for my

sheep when they were lost. You took care of yourselves and left the sheep to starve.   **Ezekiel 34:8 NLT**

Thus saith the Lord GOD; Behold, <u>I am against the shepherds</u>; and I will require my flock at their hand, and cause them to cease from feeding the flock; neither shall the shepherds feed themselves any more; for I will deliver my flock from their mouth, that they may not be meat for them.
                                                                                    Ezekiel 34:10

The prophetic judgments against the nation's pastors make it clear that God held the pastors responsible for Judah's apostasy.[29] I believe God will hold today's pastors just as responsible for the church's apostasies. Here is a list of the charges against Israel's pastors compiled from the previous verses:

- The pastors were stupid (brutish; had lost their senses).
- They no longer sought the Lord.
- They destroyed the Lord's vineyard.
- They walked all over God's people.
- They made the church desolate, not fruitful.
- They destroyed the sheep and scattered them.
- They did not visit the sheep.
- They led the sheep astray.
- They caused the people to literally wander around from place to place, forgetting their resting place (God's house).
- They abandoned the sheep and left them to be attacked.
- They didn't bother to seek out lost sheep.
- They put themselves first and neglected the sheep.
- They fed themselves, not the flock.
- They exploited the flock.

---

[29] See Jeremiah 10:19-22, 12:10-11, 23:1-4, 25:34-36, 50:6-7; Ezekiel 34:1-10.

God set forth a high standard with the writings of Jeremiah and Ezekiel, and He has yet to repent. He still considers these charges to be woefully sinful and a gross dereliction of pastoral duty. It would be wise for every New Testament pastor to study this list, judge their ministry and church, and make sure God cannot say the same things about them.

It would also be wise for Christians to avoid attending any church with a reputation similar to the list on the previous page.

2
BIBLICAL SHEPHERDING

We concluded the previous chapter by looking at corruption in the Old Testament pastorate. It would only be proper to now take a close look at *biblical* pastoring.

In the biblical context, a shepherd (not the spiritual leader, but the literal tender of a flock of wooly sheep) was a singular man assigned to care for a flock of sheep. Typically, the flock was not his own, but belonged to his father or another man much greater than himself. A shepherd was responsible for the following duties:

- Living with the fold. His life revolved around them (Exodus 3:1; Psalm 78:70-71).
- Feeding the flock (Psalm 23; Jeremiah 3:15; Ezekiel 34:23; 1 Peter 5:2; Acts 20:28).
- Leading the flock in its comings and goings (Exodus 3:1; Psalm 23).
- Keeping watch for enemies, wolves, hazards, etc. Providing general safety (Luke 2:8; 1 Peter 5:2; Acts 20:29-31).
- Providing adequate water (Psalm 23; Exodus 2:16).
- Healing the injured and sick sheep (Ezekiel 34:4).

- Pursuing the sheep that have accidentally (not intentionally) wandered out of the way (Ezekiel 34:4).
- Caring for all other needs, e.g., grooming, sheering, insecticide, etc.
- Providing a resting place for the flock (Psalm 23; Jeremiah 33:12; Ezekiel 34:15).

It is very easy to see from the list above how the pastor overseeing God's people has the same job description. A good New Testament pastor lives his life around his fold. He feeds the flock the Word of God service after service. He leads the church family through the various seasons of life and church ministry. The humble local pastor always has his keen eye out for the enemies of the flock: conniving wolves, Jezebels, troublemakers, and sexual predators.

The pastor is responsible for maintaining the refreshing waters of God's presence in the church services. He is called to check on the injured sheep and to pray for the sick. He seeks after those who have gone missing and follows up. If the pastor has fulfilled all of his duties properly, by default he will bring peace to the local congregation.

It is no wonder God chose to use the shepherd/sheep relationship to describe how both He and His local leaders care for His people. Time and again God called His executive leaders "pastors" and His people "sheep." There is such a blessing of safety, supply, training, and defense to be found in a local congregation. But because we are living in a day of lawlessness and hyper-opinionatedness, many Christians struggle to settle in a church. Their excuses can vary but they're typically just rooted in a refusal to submit. Rather than humble themselves and enjoy the blessing of a church family, they choose to live as shepherdless sheep. This lifestyle is an indication of either immaturity, ignorance, pride, or perhaps all three.

A humble and mature disciple of Jesus Christ can fit in just about anywhere the Gospel is being preached and God is being worshiped. A believer's inability to fit in a Gospel church says more about their personal immaturity than it does the church's quality. Believers should never

BIBLICAL SHEPHERDING

use their former church as an excuse to be spiritually homeless. We still need a pastor. Consider the following:

- If you thought you didn't need a pastor in Moses' day, you died a slave in Egypt.
- If you thought you didn't need a pastor in Joshua's day, you died having never received the Promised Land.
- If you thought you didn't need a pastor during the *Times of the Judges*, you stayed enslaved and oppressed by your enemies.
- If you thought you didn't need a pastor in David's day, you failed to enjoy the greatest time in Israel's history.
- If you thought you didn't need a pastor in the early days of the Church, you missed out on all the apostolic epistles being passed around and read by the local churches.
- Jesus called Himself the Good Shepherd. His sheep know His voice, and they will reject the voice of any hireling.
- You can enjoy a good sermon and still be shepherdless.
- Any person without a shepherd is described as being "scattered" and "gone astray."

A Symbiotic Relationship

In biology, symbiosis describes the mutually beneficial relationship between two different organisms. Examples include the classic relationship between the clownfish and a sea anemone and between the Egyptian plover (a bird) and a Nile crocodile. The clown fish finds safety in the poisonous tendrils of the anemone while luring predators to their doom. The Nile crocodile gets free dental care while the plover gets a free meal.

The shepherd/sheep relationship is also symbiotic. In the natural, sheep can't exist without a shepherd, but a shepherd has no livelihood without his sheep. Sheep are the only animal in the world that will never be found "in the wild." There are wild goats, wild horses, wild pigs, wild chickens, and even wild cows[1] (buffalo), but no wild sheep. Sheep have no defense mechanisms, no camouflage, and no flight speed to speak of.

Sheep can literally be lost less than a mile from their homestead. They can even accidentally kill themselves by overeating or eating the wrong plants (seriously, what kind of animal eats the wrong food or dies from overeating?).

They can't shear their own wool, which, by the way, never stops growing. Wool can actually kill sheep if it becomes too heavy with mud and debris. The unbearable weight can prohibit them from standing upright. If a sheep cannot stand, their stomach can't release digestive gases. When sheep, or any other ruminating animal, can't release the gases in their stomach, death can occur within a day. This is called *casting*. *Cast sheep* are one of the greatest threats a shepherd can face.

For these reasons, sheep are unequivocally the only animal that cannot exist without the help of mankind. They absolutely *must* have a shepherd in order to live and flourish. They *must* have a shepherd to shear their wool, protect them from predators, steer them away from poisonous weeds, and provide clean water. And yet the work a shepherd invests in his flock is richly rewarded by the sheep's wool, milk, meat, and even their ability to fertilize and restore large expanses of barren land.[2] Sheep can't exist without a shepherd, and a shepherd exists to care for his sheep.

We would do well to keep all of this in mind as we attend church, relate to the pastor, feed on the Word of God, and labor in the Kingdom. Christians need a pastor, and pastors need Christians. Christians need a pastor to shear their wool, provide clean fodder, pure water, and protect them from spiritual predators. Our lives are mutually enriched by one another. It no more benefits the shepherd to abuse his flock than it does the sheep to be offended and flee their shepherd.

---

[1] Modern cattle have been bred and domesticated far beyond their wild ancestors. There are feral (domesticated but living wild) cattle in small pockets worldwide.
[2] In ancient times, sheep were referred to as "the golden-hooved ones" because of their ability to fertilize and restore barren lands.

A Pastor's Perspective

In light of our subject and concerning the necessity of honorably departing from a local church, it may be helpful for a congregation member to understand a pastor's perspective. Pastors exist to care for the flock of God. Without sheep, we don't have a flock. Without a flock, we are without purpose. So every pastor prays that God would add to their flock.

When a new family or visitor walks in the door of our church, we humbly realize that they are an answer to prayer. (Did you hear that? We pastors see you as an answer from God to our prayers.) Our heart momentarily rejoices over the visitor—God's answer to prayer—but then reality sets in.

The reality is that we didn't pick the new family that's visiting. God did. We didn't get to vet them. God sent them. We don't know who they are, but God does. We don't know their motive; God does. We asked God to help grow our church by sending new people, and He has answered our request, but now we need His help again. Why? Because people are both the reason we do ministry and also the single greatest hassle of ministry. Ministry is hard work, and God's people often make it even harder. One pastor once quipped, "Pastoring would be great, if it weren't for all the people."

When a new family visits a church, the experienced pastor begins to ask questions that, to be honest, can sound a little paranoid. Questions like: Are they here because they're hungry for God or are they here to spy out our liberty? Are they friend or foe? Have they come to help build up or to tear down? Is this a Peter or a Judas? Is this a Deborah or a Jezebel? Are they here looking for discipleship or looking to grow their business? Do they want to advance the Kingdom or advance their political career? Do they want to help me with my ministry or use me to jumpstart their own ministry? Just exactly how much spiritual baggage are they bringing with them? This may all sound a little cynical, but anyone who has pastored longer than six months can probably attest to having many of these thoughts.

The Apostle Paul warned the elders at Ephesus that after his departing grievous wolves would enter in, not sparing the flock. And not only wolves from the outside, Paul also prophesied that "of your own selves shall men arise, speaking perverse things, to draw away disciples after them."[3] According to Paul, pastors get to deal with wolves on the outside and perverse people on the inside. When you consider that Paul's warning was really the Holy Spirit preparing those leaders for what was destined to come, it's easy to understand why pastors might be a little suspicious of new people.

To further complicate matters, building a congregation isn't like building a professional sports team. Pastors don't have professional recruiters out in the local churches scouting the other congregations for talent, waving huge incentive contracts in front of them. The only recruiting God permits is either through evangelism or by personal invitation.

I realize there are some very unethical hirelings out there that float from church to church with the intent of stealing sheep away, but thankfully that is the exception and not the rule.[4] But it should be mentioned that there may be nothing more frustrating, infuriating, and hurtful to a pastor than to see a visitor come into their church and, with selfish motives, move among the beloved sheep only to draw away disciples after themselves. Don't be this type of hireling sheep-thief. Every community has them. Mark them and have nothing to do with them.[5]

When a new family walks into a church, the pastor sees potential. He sees potential help. He sees a potential prayer partner. A potential children's department worker. A potential worship leader. A potential elder. A potential giver. A potential Timothy. A potential Silas. Or . . . a potential nitpicker. A potential complainer. A potential gossip. A potential traitor. A potential wolf. A potential Judas. A potential Absalom. All of this runs through the mind of a pastor as he continues to obey God in the divine

---

[3] Acts 20:29-30
[4] As a word of warning, I would never leave a proven local pastor for some drifter-preacher-hireling. It won't end well.
[5] Romans 16:17

calling to feed and lead the flock of God. And to be perfectly honest, we have to treat everybody the same service after service while we prove who is who and what is what.

If you are just joining a new church, don't become impatient if the pastor has yet to use you. Know that he has his assignment from God, and he has probably already prayerfully established protocols for assimilating new believers and new members. These protocols were more than likely birthed out of trial, error, successes, failures, the Bible, and the leading of God's Spirit. Please don't think you, as the new member, are the special exemption to these protocols.

If your new pastor is a wise pastor, he's going to first prove you to see what you're made of. Also keep in mind, he was probably doing just fine before you ever arrived at his church. He also knows you most certainly know nothing yet about the history of his church, where they are coming from, where they are going, what their vision is, what their church culture is, what battles they just fought and won (or lost), what ditch they're having to currently lean against, or what their God-ordained assignment is.

Furthermore, if the church is prospering and running efficiently, the pastor risks disrupting a good thing by using you prematurely. Instead, be patient and establish yourself. It is God who promotes one and sits another down.[6] Catch the pastor's heart. Learn the church's culture and verbiage. And show yourself to be teachable and humble. Be faithful! God will soon direct the pastor to use you in his church and among his sheep.

---

[6] Psalm 75:6-7

3
GOD PICKS YOUR CHURCH

Please bear with me now as the next few paragraphs will discuss a bit of theology. I find it necessary to do so because so many Christians are now embracing the lie that church attendance is optional. Though what follows might be a bit tedious, I want to theologically defend our need for both church attendance and church membership.

Perhaps you've heard the modern mantra: *The Church isn't a building*. This is accurate, but some have taken this sentiment so far as to argue, "Since the Church isn't a building, I don't have to *go* to 'church' to *have* church. I can have church anywhere I am." Though there is some biblical truth here, you can't help but hear a bit of rebellion in such a statement. Plus, the full doctrine is not that simple.

The Bible's full teaching on church attendance is held in doctrinal tension. What tension? Well, the Bible presents the Body of Christ as both visible and invisible. It is both supernatural and natural. Individual Christians are the Temple of God, but we are also commanded to meet corporately and grow together *unto* a holy temple in the Lord.[1] Church members meet in the House of God, but as lively stones we are built up

---

[1] See 1 Corinthians 3:16, 6:19; Hebrews 10:25; Ephesians 2:21.

into a spiritual house.² So it's both. The Church isn't a building, but when the saints of God meet together in a facility for the purpose of worshiping and honoring the King of kings, that building becomes the House of God. If Christians never assemble and don't have a church to call home, they are spiritually homeless.

Theology uses two fancier terms to describe this dual nature: ***incarnate*** and ***discarnate***.

> **Incarnate**: *possessing a physical body, as in Jesus Christ, the incarnate God, or God in the flesh.*

The doctrine of *the Incarnation*³ is the foundation stone of Christianity; for without the Word becoming flesh, possessing a physical body, dwelling among us, and dying to redeem us, we would still be altogether dead in our trespasses and sins.

The Incarnation makes Christianity unique among all religions of the world. No other religion in history has ever dared to suggest that a god would become man (on the contrary, many pagan religions are consumed with turning men into gods). The centrality of *the Incarnation* in Christianity indicates to us that God *is* concerned with physical bodies; after all, God was given a body in order to redeem us. This is important because it reveals that not everything in the Kingdom is meant to be mystical, spiritual, or ethereal.

The Kingdom involves a lot of "boots on the ground" practical realities. In fact, even our own eternity will be spent in a tangible, glorified body. Though we will all put off this mortal body in death, the "glory" of the Resurrection is the promise of a new *glorified* body. As one theologian observed, "It seems as though the Bible is not content with a bodiless eternity." This just further reveals that God's Kingdom places some emphasis on tangible bodies.

---

² 1 Peter 2:5
³ *The Incarnation* is the belief that Jesus Christ, the second person of the Trinity, assumed human form in the virgin birth, and is therefore fully God and fully man.

This is critical to our subject because the term *incarnate* is also applied theologically to the fellowship of a local church body. A local church body is made of tangible humans assembling their tangible bodies together in one tangible location. In this regard, we *are* the incarnate body of Christ in the earth today. We are His hands, His feet, and His mouth to those around us. Paul was very clear on this in 1 Corinthians 12:12-27. When we, the individual eyes, ears, nose, arms, hands, and feet come together, we become the incarnate body of Christ. When certain members choose to stay home and skip service, they force their local church body to operate as an amputee. Unfortunately, many churches have to function as severe amputees every service. Please don't handicap your church through absenteeism. Be a part of your local incarnate church.

Discarnate: *without a physical body, like an apparition or a ghost.*

God the Father is a spirit and therefore does *not* have a physical body. The Holy Spirit also does *not* have a physical body. Jesus Christ, on the other hand, was given a human body in the virgin birth and then received a glorified body at His resurrection. I find it pretty wild to consider that the Eternal God has now inhabited two tangible bodies. These bodies were and are technically the bodies of Christ, but the Church is also called the Body of Christ[4] (there's that doctrinal tension again). The worldwide body of Christian believers—the Church, the whole family in Heaven[5]—is a supernatural and discarnate Body. It is not tangible. It is into this discarnate Body we were all baptized at the new birth and made to drink of the same Spirit.[6]

I hope you're still with me. To review: The Body of Christ is both *incarnate* (the local church) and *discarnate* (the whole family in Heaven). It is both local and worldwide. It is simultaneously natural and super-

---

[4] See Ephesians 1:22-23 and 5:30.
[5] Ephesians 3:15
[6] 1 Corinthians 12:13

natural, visible and invisible. The Body of Christ is comprised of individual temples coming together to be built up into a spiritual temple.[7]

It is true that being a member of a local *incarnate* church body doesn't get us into Heaven, but being a member of the *discarnate* spiritual Body of Christ should really make us want to assemble together. So here is where we get down to the heart of the problem: How can a Christian claim to be part of the invisible Church without being part of the visible church? Or to ask it another way: How can we expect to fellowship with the Head of the Church (Jesus) when we never fellowship with His Body (a local body of believers)?

These are important questions because we are living in a day where technology makes discarnate rebellion easy. Western church attendance is in rapid decline and the convenience of technology is partially to blame. Though the internet and video streaming now allow the Gospel minister to get their message online and out to the entire world, this also assists the lukewarm Christian in absenteeism. How ironic. The same technology that can propel a small country preacher to a worldwide audience can also destroy one of his own fold who refuses to be part of the local church.

Now more than ever, the Christian who was looking for an excuse to not go to church has one: *I can just stream online.* I can tell you as a pastor who streams four services a week from our church in Tennessee: we don't do it so you can stay home! We don't use technology to create spectators. We use technology to disciple those who want to be in the House of God but are unable to due to work, sickness, or travel.

The New Testament commands every believer (including ministers) to have a church and assemble together. It's not a suggestion. It's a command for every Christian. No one is so special that they're above this commandment, not even the missionary.

---

[7] 1 Peter 2:5

Not forsaking our own assembling[8] together, as is the habit of some, but encouraging one another; and all the more as you see the day drawing near.   Hebrews 10:25 NASB

According to the author of Hebrews, some Christians are in the habit of forsaking the incarnate Body of Christ. Forsaking is a strong word in the original Greek. It means *to totally abandon, to desert, to leave behind.* Have you done this? Have you totally abandoned the local assembly? Have you deserted your church? Have you been deceived into thinking you can fellowship with Jesus without going to church? Or maybe you've only developed the habit of skipping church. Maybe you are able to go to church but still choose to attend online. Why? Don't allow technology to *excarnate* the Body of Christ, that is, strip it of its tangibility and human interaction.

God ordained for us, the Body of Christ, to interact with one another, actually serving together, praying together, rejoicing together, weeping together, and suffering together. Technology can be a blessing, just so long as it isn't used to debone the Body of Christ. There is a strong argument to be made that digital churches are not strong churches. Just like an online marriage is doomed to fail if husband and wife never come together, likewise online churches are destined to fail if the believers never come together.

This is all just a fancy theological way of saying that if you call yourself a Christian, you need to be planted in a strong local church. Period.

Where Am I Called?

As a pastor, I'm often asked, "How do I find a good church?" Though I understand the sentiment, we must understand that just because a church is a "good church," that doesn't mean it's the one God has ordained for you. A better question might be, "How do I find the church God has called me to?"

---

[8] Greek *episynagoge*. We see the root word is *synagogue*. Here, translated as a gathering together in one place and the religious assembly of Christians.

We must be aware of how much culture can creep in and pervert God's Kingdom. As Westerners, we've been taught from a young age to make everything in life about us. Our upbringing bombarded us with questions like:

- What do *you* want to be when you grow up?
- What college do *you* want to go to?
- Where do *you* want to work?
- When do *you* want to get married?
- How many kids do *you* want to have?

The demand of these questions forced us to always have an answer, but no one ever seemed to teach us what the right answers were. Sometimes I think we made things up just because we didn't have an answer when we were put on the spot. The only problem with these questions and their answers is that, whether intentionally or unintentionally, they omit God and His will. In fact, questions like these don't even acknowledge Him or His Kingdom.

The biblical question isn't, "What do *you* want to be when you grow up?" but rather, "What do you believe *God* would have you do with the rest of the life *He* has given you?" It doesn't matter where we want to go to college. We ought to be asking, "God, do You even want me to go to college, and if so, where?" Likewise, we shouldn't ask someone, "How many kids do you want?" because all that matters is, "How many children do you believe God wants to give you?" If these adjusted questions have caused your mind to tilt, you're probably more Western in some of your perspectives than you are biblical.

This constant line of self-centric questioning inadvertently trains even the best-intentioned Christians to erroneously assume that all decisions in life are theirs to make, including where they go to church. Afterall, if my career is my choice, if my schooling is my choice, if my major is my choice, if my spouse is my choice, why wouldn't where I go to church also be my choice? Instead of seeking God for where *He* would have us put down roots and serve, many Christians are still asking the wrong questions. Questions like: What are you looking for in a church? And how long are the church services? Or how big is the singles group?

Asking the wrong questions will always produce useless answers. It's like being low on gas, looking for a desperately needed gas station, but only asking how clean the bathrooms are. What does one have to do with the other?

I was once a youth pastor for three years in a relatively small five-year-old church plant. When my pastor asked me to take over the position, he expressed to me his extreme frustration with God's people. He related to me how before my arrival, numerous families had visited and felt the genuine call of God to join the church. Initially they were very excited. However, upon learning how small the youth group was (less than 10 kids at the time), they decided to disobey God and go across town to a different church with a larger youth group. The common excuse was, "We really feel called to this church, but our kids need a good youth group. So, we are going to sacrifice this calling for our kids." To which my pastor protested to me in frustration, "No! They're going to sacrifice their kids." He then continued, "Do you know how large our youth group would be if all of those families had decided to obey God and stay here? We'd have a youth group the size they're looking for, plus they'd all still be in the will of God!"

For these families, the youth group was the selling point for their new church, not the divine will of God. Is God against our kids? Absolutely not. Is He against a big youth group? Absolutely not. Those things are great, and may every church be able to have one if God wants them to have one, but a large youth group does not a great church make. God doesn't assign us to any church based on the secondary ministries they offer. Choosing a church based on secondary ministries is tantamount to walking by sight. What if God calls you to a church without a youth ministry just so you can be the one to help the pastor pioneer it?

Honestly, many American Christians now treat finding a church almost like trying to find a place to eat on Friday night. Imagine a Sunday morning conversation between a husband and wife looking for a new church (or maybe a restaurant):

"What are you up for?" the husband begins.

"I don't know. How far do you want to drive?" his wife replies.

"It depends," he adds.

"On what?" she asks.

"On whether or not they offer anything for the kids."

"Oh! I found something," looking on her smartphone.

Intrigued, he asks, "Oh? Does it say how long it would take to get in and out?"

"No . . . I don't see anything," she replies.

He suddenly remembers a recent conversation, "What was the name of that one place the Joneses said they really enjoyed?"

"I don't know which one you're talking about."

Frustrated, "Sure you do! The other day when we were talking to them."

"What are you talking about?" Then, suddenly redirecting, she adds, "Hey, why don't we just try that new place in town everyone's been talking about? I saw their advertisement on Facebook."

"Ok. That'd probably just be easier anyway," he concedes and off they go.

And that is how the decision is too frequently made—"That'd probably just be easier anyway." Shame on any Christian looking for the easier way to serve God. Have we forgotten that serving God still requires a sacrifice?

Unfortunately, this is a Westernized conversation, and it really sounds like our make-believe couple is looking for a restaurant rather than a House of God to serve in and raise their family.

Regardless, these are not Kingdom-minded questions. Maybe, just maybe, somewhere in that imaginary conversation the Christian couple in search of a new church might think to ask, "What does this church actually believe? Are they focused on the Great Commission?" and, "Do they maintain the presence of God there?" or hopefully, "Is this where God is calling us to put down roots and serve?"

So what questions should you ask if you're trying to find a church? That's a good question, and I'm glad you asked. How about:

- Where is God calling me (and my family) to serve Him?
- Who has God assigned to be my pastor?
- Is the Bible being faithfully taught there?
- Is the Holy Spirit free to move there?
- Are the other congregation members being challenged and changed there?

Why God Picks Your Church

Here's the truth that may seem extremely foreign to the modern Western Christian: biblically, you don't get to "pick" your church—God does. If that seems foreign to you, fear not! You're not alone. It's apparently also foreign to a lot of pastors, who work so hard to market, advertise, and reinvent their churches in hopes of drawing more people. I guess they forgot Jesus declared that He would build the Church and that when He is lifted up, He will draw all men unto Himself. The sooner pastors remember these Bible promises, the sooner they can stop wasting time, money, and effort on marketing strategies, fads, and gimmicks.

I've come to realize that if I will seek God and make my church what He wants it to be, He will draw the people He wants there. I recognize not everyone in my region is called to my church, and I am perfectly content with that fact.

> **[18]But now God has placed the members, each one of them, in the body, just as He desired. [27]Now you are Christ's body, and individual members of it.   1 Corinthians 12:18, 27 NASB**

Paul revealed that God places every member of the incarnate Body exactly where He desires them (assuming they follow and obey). But why? Why don't we get to choose where we go to church? Upon being born again, God equips every Christian with different graces and abilities necessary to fulfill their predestined calling.[9] He designed those unique giftings and graces to find their fullest manifestation in a divinely appointed local church.

> **[5]So we being many, are one body in Christ, and every one members one of another. [6]Having then gifts according to the grace that is given to us, . . .**   **Romans 12:5-6a**

God assigns us to the exact church that just happens to need what God has given us. And lest we get puffed up in pride over the divine graces God has given us to help the local church, keep in mind that it will take the ministry of the pastor to help develop them. Though the pastor needs us to fulfill the potential of the church, we also need him to fulfill the potential that God has placed in us. (There's that symbiosis again.)

Unfortunately, this spiritual truth somehow manages to escape many believers and many modern churches, who consequently, resort to marketing techniques to grow their church, adjusting their message and ministry to "reach" the "non-customer." Rather than allowing the Lord to *build* His local church with the graces and giftings of the people He calls and assigns there, too many churches choose to draw a crowd through secular techniques. Basically, secular churches tend to draw anybody and everybody, paying no attention to what God purposes to do with those genuinely assigned to their church.

If God allowed us to pick our church, then personal taste, emotions, favorite culture, comfort, and the sin nature would manage to have a say, and we'd end up in a church that allowed us to serve God on our terms.

A Christian has no more of a say in where he attends church than a soldier has a say in which military base he has been stationed at. Can you imagine any soldier in any army of the world telling their commanding officer where they're going to be stationed come deployment? Laughable! Or when they will or won't show up for duty? Preposterous! Are we not

---

[9] See Ephesians 4:7.

soldiers in God's Army? Is Jesus Christ not the Lord of Hosts? Are we not His to command? We would be wise to say, "Here am I, Lord. Send me where You need me."

God Is The Master Strategist

The Body of Christ is truly a body. It requires every member to be present and functioning at their optimal ability in order to accomplish the assignment with which they have been tasked. God knows exactly where He *wants* every believer; it is His Body after all. More particularly, God knows exactly where He *needs* us. He knows *which* people have *what* giftings and graces and *where* they are precisely needed. He also knows the anointing He has placed upon every local pastor and what that anointing can do in the lives of those called to that church.

> **He makes the whole body fit together perfectly. As each part does its own special work, it helps the other parts grow, so that the whole body is healthy and growing and full of love.**
> **Ephesians 4:16 NLT**

God is so gracious to assign every local body all the parts and abilities necessary to fulfill the vision He has assigned them. Not everyone is an eye, for where would the hearing be? And not everyone is a nose, for where would the tasting be? Nor is everyone a leg or an arm. Instead, the Lord brings together diverse people from diverse backgrounds with diverse abilities and fitly joins them together in the body of a local church.

Though this divine model requires great faith, when followed, it glorifies God and accomplishes a great work for Christ. It makes the seemingly impossible, God-ordained assignment possible because the burden of spiritual responsibility is placed upon every member according to their divine graces. Of the eyes, sight is required. Of the feet, locomotion is required. Of the ears, hearing is required, and so forth.

Furthermore, these members don't just give of their individual abilities, they also receive of the other members' graces. The ear is benefited by the eyes' sight, and the eyes are benefited by the legs' locomotion, and so on. Each body part benefits the other and each ability is necessary, but it should be abundantly evident that each member must be present if the local church is to function effectively.

As a pastor, I am eager to help people get to the church God has called them to. I'm not interested in stealing any shepherd's sheep. If I can perceive a family or individual isn't called to my church, I will do all that I can to connect them to another church in town that may be more fitting. (Admittedly, this requires being friends with a lot of different churches, but that's not a bad thing.)

If I'm a Toyota repair shop, I need Toyota parts. Ford parts, though wonderful, robust, and valuable, won't work with what I'm doing. They belong at the Ford repair shop down the road. And while some pastors seem keen on collecting as many automotive parts as possible (whether they need them or not or know what to do with them or not), I have learned to be content with the parts God allots to me. Contentment takes great faith.

Likewise, if sheep don't fit at my church, that means another church is missing them, their giftings, and their help. It also means that retaining them is selfish and only serves to hurt the Kingdom (though it may boost my numbers and make me look good). I believe that if God can trust me to help His people find where they belong, He will send me the people I need.

I Didn't Like God's Choice

When God spoke to me to move to the Midwest to attend Bible school, I was a little concerned because I didn't know what church I was to attend. The city where I was moving to was large and there were many options, but I spent months praying about the move and everything involved with it. Three months before my move, I visited the city for a few days to "spy out the land," look for an apartment, visit the school, and interview for a job.

One afternoon I was in a hotel room shaving my face in preparation for a job interview I had lined up. As I was shaving, I spoke to the Lord again about what church He would have me to attend while in school. I remember my words very vividly, "Lord, here I am 'spying out the land' and preparing to move for Bible school. Everywhere I've ever gone I've taught Your people that they need a church and they need a pastor. I'm about to leave both to come here for a Bible school, but I don't know where You'd have me go to church. That makes me a hypocrite, Lord, and I don't want to be a hypocrite. Please speak to me about a church." I had no sooner prayed these words when the Spirit of God spoke to me and clearly said, "Get among the Assemblies (of God)."

This was not the answer I was expecting. This was not a favorable answer for me. I was not Assemblies of God. This was not my denominational background. I argued a bit with the Lord over it, but before I was done shaving, I had consecrated myself to His will, and I determined to find an Assemblies of God church.

I visited a few Assemblies of God churches, then I made an appointment with the district superintendent's office to get their recommendations. The superintendent was out of town, but his wife was gracious to meet with me. She recommended a certain church that they considered to be the flagship and crown jewel for their district, so that's where I went. And that's where I met my wife. The Assemblies was *not* my choice, but it was God's, and it continues to benefit me richly. We must learn that when it comes to our church assignment, Father knows best!

But How Do I Find My God-Ordained Church?

God is so gracious. He knows how well we do and don't hear from Him. He wants us to be in the right church more than we want to be there, so we can trust Him to get us there. Ideally, it would be great if God would speak to us clearly in prayer, but that just isn't always the case. Even in my situation with Bible school and attending the Assemblies of God church, God didn't tell me which one. He simply said, "Get among the Assemblies of God." I had to do some research and start visiting. Below is a general list of things I recommend to any believer in their search for the church where

God has called them to. It should be noted that all of these can still be done from the safety of your current church.

- **Prayer**—Christians must begin every Kingdom endeavor with a framework of prayer. The Lord wants to lead us in paths of righteousness, and the Holy Spirit wants to lead us into all truth. Prayer begins to make that all possible. Prayer opens up supernatural leadings and divine connections. Pray that God would lead and guide you to the right church.
- **Research**—This can include asking your current pastor for recommendations, talking to people about their church, searching the internet for churches in your area, and calling different churches. The internet should grant you access to a church's doctrinal statement and even allow you to listen to some of the pastor's sermons and teaching style. A lot of church options can be eliminated in the research stage.
- **Visiting**—After prayer and research, it's time to actually visit a church. If you've done thorough research before visiting the church, the chances of being shocked or taken aback by the nature or content of a service are slim to none. Though a church can be visited virtually online, this can never take the place of actually being there in person and judging the spirit of the service, the heart of a message, and the quality of the disciples. It's one thing to see the pastor online; it's another thing to rub elbows with his disciples. It is also advisable to visit more than one service in order to get a better feel for the full extent of the church's various ministries. Visiting in person will allow the Spirit of God on the inside of you to bear witness with you concerning whether or not this is *the* church for you. Remember, where you go to church is the Holy Spirit's decision, not yours.

As an extra help, what follows is a list of six things to look for in a strong local church. It should be apparent that none of these criteria have anything to do with a denominational title or the size of the youth group. When visiting churches, we need to look for spiritual fruit, not necessarily titles, associations, or secondary ministry offerings. Here are six critical fruit:

1. **They preach Jesus Christ and Him crucified, the only way to the Father** (1 Corinthians 2:2; John 14:6). This is non-negotiable.

2. **They preach/teach the whole counsel of God's Word,** not just the feel-good parts. God's Word is profitable for doctrine, reproof, correction, and instruction (2 Timothy 3:16).

3. **They preach against sin**, especially your sin. If sin is not confronted, darkness wins. One of the pastor's jobs is to tell people in what way their life is wrong (2 Timothy 4:2 AMPC).[10]

4. **They are active in evangelism** (Mark 16:15). This is the first half of the Great Commission. Any church not endeavoring to reach the lost is derelict in their Christian duty.

5. **They are active in discipleship** (Matthew 28:19-20). This is the second half of the Great Commission. Discipleship means Christians are growing and changing into the image of Jesus Christ.

6. **They have a fearless pastor** (2 Timothy 1:7). You want to find a shepherd who fears no one, especially you. His obligation and allegiance must be to God Almighty and the Lord Jesus Christ.

Any church with this kind of fruit will go a long way toward changing your life and helping you finish your race. Any church lacking even two

---

[10] The Holy Bible: The Amplified Bible (Classic). 1987. 2015. La Habra, CA: The Lockman Foundation.

or three of these criteria will be seriously suspect. The more of these you can find in a church, the safer you will be there.

Visiting a new church might be a little intimidating, but just remember these are your brothers and sisters in Christ. View it as a gathering of family you've never met.

4
ROOT BALL CHRISTIANS

If you've ever been to a home improvement, warehouse-type store, no doubt you've seen one of those trees with their root masses securely bundled in a burlap sack. This burlap-bundled root mass is called a root ball. It's a bizarre sight to observe one of these trees, standing tall and upright, leaning against a fence, supported by a little root ball base not much larger than a basketball.

As it turns out, a root-balled tree can live for weeks, even months, sitting on a concrete parking lot so long as it receives adequate water and sunshine. This may sound like a positive thing, but we must make the distinction between a tree merely existing and a tree growing and flourishing. The truth is the tree was never designed to live in a root bag. Even the arborist who dug up the tree at the nursery and bundled its roots for transport never intended for the tree to continue living like that.

When the arborist at the nursery dug up the tree, it was with the intention that at some point someone would purchase the tree, take it home, dig a proper hole, remove the burlap root bag, and plant the tree in its new environment. It is only after the tree has been planted that it can begin to grow and flourish again.

Though a root ball can survive while bound by burlap, the minerals vital for growth are only available in the soil. And even if one were to water the root ball with fertilizer water, the root-balled tree is rootbound, meaning its roots are also stunted from growing. Stunted root growth means stunted tree growth. If the tree happens to be a fruit-bearing tree, it also means the tree will be unable to produce proper fruit.

As a pastor, I have observed many Christians behaving just like a root ball tree. They leave one ministry, having uprooted themselves from where they were planted, and they arrive at my church bound with a root bag over their heart. They scope us out, investigate our ministry to see what we're about, hang out for a few weeks or months, but never take the root bag off and get planted. Because they never root themselves, they are often easily offended, distracted, or lured away. Their root-bagged heart allows them to just bounce on down the road to the next church and begin the same cycle anew. Some believers have even operated this way for decades. I call them *root ball Christians*. They live. They exist. But because of their non-committal attitudes and practices, they will never be able to grow, flourish, or bear meaningful fruit. They will certainly never be able to finish their race for God.

Don't be a root ball Christian. Figure out where God wants you to serve. Take the burlap guards off your heart, dig a good hole, and get planted as soon as possible. Begin to grow, flourish, and bear fruit. If you're not sure where you belong yet, it would be wise to obey the old maxim: Bloom where you're planted. Be like the righteous in Psalm 1:3 (emphasis mine):

And he shall <u>be like a tree planted</u> by the rivers of water, that bringeth forth his fruit in his season; his leaf also shall not wither; and whatsoever he doeth shall prosper.

Transplant Shock

When a tree is transplanted, it will experience what is called *transplant shock*. This arboreal phenomenon refers to the negative effects a plant or tree will experience when it is replanted. Transplanting a plant always results in some initial loss or damage to the *root system* that will in turn cause a loss in the *shoot system*,[1] e.g., leaves might wilt or fall off, a few branches may die, or there could be an abrupt loss of flowers or fruit.

A tree's roots are responsible for absorbing the water and nutrients necessary for the production of the stems, branches, leaves, flowers, and fruit. When any part of the root mass is damaged or destroyed, it will negatively affect whatever part of the *shoot system* those roots were supporting with its lifegiving sap. This is unavoidable and is to be expected. If the *root system* is extremely damaged, it is possible for the plant to totally die.

However, pruning limbs or branches at the time of transplant can alleviate a burden from the *root system* by removing the burden of unsustainable branches. This will increase the odds of the plant's survival by allowing the roots to focus on their new growth and not on supporting unnecessary branches or leaves. Pruning also prepares the remaining branches for their new growth once the *transplant shock* has subsided.

One final word from the amazing world of science as it relates to transplanting trees: plants with a shallow *root system* typically have a lot of trouble surviving a transplant. This should encourage us to be deeply rooted and eschew the life of a shallow believer.

Christian Transplants

Hopefully, your heart has been processing this brief lesson in horticulture as an allegory for your Christian walk. The same thing will happen to us when we are transplanted from one church to another, and I think we intuitively know this. Honestly, it can be a little scary. It is scary because departing the church we are currently planted in requires us to walk away from so much that is familiar to us: the pastor, the church family, the worship, the doctrine, the culture, the expectations, etc.

The longer we have been planted in our church, the harder it can be to leave because our roots seem impossibly deep. We may fear what the future holds or question how the future can be better than where we currently are, but I believe that's part of every God-ordained move—it will

---

[1] The shoot system includes anything that grows above ground. It includes the stem, leaves, flower, fruit, etc.

require us to trust God. If God is really in our move, it will take God to ensure our transplant is successful. If our roots are healthy and deep, only God will be able to safely dig us up and transplant us. If we can move without God, do we really have the right to declare it was His plan?

A church change can also be scary because we realize that this spiritual transplant comes with its own kind of pruning. We may not have limbs or branches pruned, but our church responsibilities will get cut back. Our connections get pruned. Our influence gets pruned. Our notoriety may even get pruned. But all of this is necessary for our church transplant to be healthy and successful.

It is only proper that upon landing at a new church we give ourselves a season to overcome *transplant shock*. We should no more expect to be immediately given the same responsibilities we had at our former church any more than a newly transplanted tree should expect to bloom new flowers or bear new fruit the same day it's planted. Being transplanted will require us to take a season to develop new growth in our roots before we can ever expect new growth in our fruit. Or to put it another way, we shouldn't expect to be used at the new church until we first catch the pastor's or church's vision and prove ourselves faithful.

Christians cannot be promoted without being planted. Being planted is the beginning of faithfulness, and God only promotes the faithful. Paul said he was promoted into ministry only *after* he was counted faithful.[2] He maintained this high standard by passing it down to Timothy when he commanded the young pastor to take what he had been taught by Paul and only commit it to "faithful men, who shall be able to teach others also."[3] Timothy was taught to only trust the faithful. Faithfulness qualifies you to teach and lead others. Root ball Christians are not trustworthy. As a pastor, I cannot build a church with root ball Christians any more than an apple farmer can build an orchard out of root-balled apple trees.

---

[2] 1 Timothy 1:12
[3] 2 Timothy 2:2

Root Ball Deception And Excuses

Many times, root ball Christians deceive themselves by blaming their church for their lack of growth or inability to "get anything out of the service." Other excuses include, "We're just not being fed here," or "I'm not being used here." While such scenarios like this do genuinely occur in dead churches, this isn't true everywhere. There are exceptions to every rule, but it is unwise to always assume we are *that* exception just so we can break the rule.

If you happen to be having trouble at your new church, first judge yourself and see if you've removed the burlap sack and put down any roots yet. When a thirsty tree puts down roots, it can't help but suck up and absorb *everything* the soil has to offer, and it's more than happy to do so. As Proverbs says, "but to the hungry soul every bitter thing is sweet."[4] If you're having trouble putting down roots in your new church, you have to ask yourself why. You must figure out what's causing your hang-up so you can put down healthy roots and grow. Your spiritual health depends on it.

It should be evident that no two churches are the same. God doesn't need them to be the same. Yes, churches all aspire to be like Jesus Christ and to honor Him and His Word, but even in pursuing that aim, it will be impossible for every church to do so identically. One of the counterintuitive beauties of biblical Christianity is that the more we all aspire to be Christ-like, the more individualistic we become because we each become the fullness of what He predestined. The inverse of this truth is amusingly ironic: the more the world seeks to be individualistic, the more they all end up looking alike.

As we've previously seen, God has placed different callings, giftings, graces, and assignments upon each pastor and their congregation. Likewise, each church will endure their own unique attacks and opposition from the enemy. These truths are demonstrated by John's writings to the *Seven Churches of the Apocalypse* in Revelation chapters 2 and 3.

---

[4] Proverbs 27:7b

ROOT BALL CHRISTIANS

Those seven churches were all within approximately 30 miles of the next closest church. That's not a long distance by today's standards, but in 1st Century Asia Minor, that could be a two-day journey. As Jesus addressed each of the churches, their different strengths, weaknesses, oppositions, and sins were revealed. Though six of the seven churches were complimented by Jesus in some way or another, the Ephesian church was in danger of being shut down. Sardis was on spiritual life support. Pergamos was struggling with bad doctrine. Thyatira was being internally corrupted by a resident Jezebel who fancied herself a prophetess. Two of the churches (Smyrna and Philadelphia) were facing persecution, and the Laodiceans were so deluded in their self-estimation, they couldn't see that their lukewarmness made Jesus want to puke.

Any 1st Century Christian changing membership from one of these churches to any of the others would probably have been in for a rude awakening. I'm sure they probably squawked and squeaked like many modern believers saying things like, "We just can't seem to find a church like we're used to," or "This church is so different from where we're from." Maybe, "We're looking for an Ephesian-type church." Or, "We're of the Smyrna faith tradition." The truth is, each of these seven churches were distinct and unique, yet Jesus was actively speaking to each and every one of them.

You can't forget, that God knows the church He is sending you to will be unlike the church you came from. And that is probably why He sent you there, assuming, of course, He was the one who moved you. It's ironic that while some Christians complain, "I can't find a good church," many pastors opine, "I can't get any good sheep."

If God has called you to leave one church and to be planted in another, it is for good reason. He knows the two churches have many differences, but don't forget they have a lot in common, too. Things like Christ crucified, the authority of the Bible, the Word preached, praise and worship, communion, prayer, the fellowship of the believers, and the presence of God. Hopefully, what they have in common can suffice you.

Have you ever considered that perhaps the new church has things you need that the previous church didn't? It could be that God is reassigning you there to add things to you that could not be learned or obtained at your previous church. So get in there, take off your root bag, and put down roots as soon as possible. Only the Lord truly knows what you're missing by living bundled in fear and reluctance.

Lifelong Root Balls

Even the strongest churches led by great pastors will have congregation members that never seem to "get it." These members just don't ever seem to grow, develop, mature, or change. When every other church member is lost in the presence of God during worship, Johnny Root Ball is bored and looking around.

While everyone else is frantically taking notes from the sermon and being challenged by the preaching and teaching of sound doctrine, Sister Root Ball is bored, critical of the delivery style, and claims she isn't being fed.

When the faithful saints are eager to show up for a work detail or an evangelistic outreach, the so-called "Rev." Root Ball still isn't sure if he totally agrees with the church's direction just yet.

These kinds of people are deceived. For whatever reason, they refuse to remove the burlap sack from their hearts and put down roots. They fail to see that such a fearful attitude will keep them stunted spiritual pygmies. When it's evident by the fruit in the rest of the congregation's lives that their church is good ground and their pastor is a righteous and just farmer, then the problem must be in the heart of the disgruntled sheep.

How is it they don't grow or bear fruit when everyone else so readily does? How? Easy. They're still just root-balled up. They have yet to remove the burlap veil from their heart. And so, when offenses come, they'll be able to easily move on to the next church that, likewise, won't be good enough for them. This will more than likely be the pattern for the rest of their lives. They will fancy themselves spiritual oak trees but fail to see the reality that they're only aged root ball saplings. Aging, but never maturing.

ROOT BALL CHRISTIANS

Don't be like them. Don't be a root ball Christian. Trust that God knows what He is doing when He assigns you to a church. Remove that burlap guard from your heart, put down some roots, and grow, grow, grow!

5
GENERAL DOS AND DON'TS
(When Leaving A Church)

It has been observed and taught by many great ministers of the Gospel that how you leave one place is exactly how you will arrive at the next place. Likewise, how you end one relationship is exactly how you will start a new relationship. For this reason, we must be ever cautious how we conclude something old. This includes beginning a new phase in our Christian service as we conclude the last assignment given.

In my research for this book I decided to poll fellow pastors to see what their experience has been regarding sheep departure and more specifically, carnal sheep departure. I created a simple questionnaire and asked the respondents the following questions:

1. How long have you been pastoring?
2. Where have you pastored?
3. Have you ever seen a Christian leave your church dishonorably and then prosper or succeed in life?[1]

---

[1] Success and prosperity mean different things to different people. Jesus asked, "Why gain the world and lose your soul?" Here, it is understood to mean walking

GENERAL DOS AND DON'TS

4. Please list the excuses people have given when they leave dishonorably.
5. If you have seen a Christian leave dishonorably and succeed, please explain why you think they may have been able to do so.
6. When a church member leaves your church, what is the one thing that you would request of them before they leave?

Though admittedly, my questionnaire did not meet the rigors of highly scientific polling, the results are very telling. Consider the following:

- Over 50 pastors responded.
- The average pastoral respondent had pastored for 23 years.
- This represents over 1,200 years of pastoral experience.
- Seven denominations were represented.
- The responding pastors were from 11 countries and 16 different states throughout the USA.
- 74% of these pastors declared they had never seen a church member leave dishonorably and then succeed in life.

Seventy-four percent! This pastoral witness alone should make us pause when we believe it's time to change churches. If nearly 75% of pastors testify that they've *never* seen someone leave their church dishonorably and be able to prosper in life, we should really slow down and evaluate our motives and methods when the idea of changing churches enters our mind.

Possible Reasons For Success

With 74% of the pastors reporting no Christian success after dishonorable departures, it might be interesting to look into what permitted success for the remaining 26%. Thankfully some pastors who responded to our poll

---

with God, enjoying His blessing, favor, and promotion upon your life and family. We do not mean simple natural prosperity or success.

offered their explanation for such scenarios. There were only two reasons given to explain how a Christian might leave a church in a sinful manner and still prosper:

1. They were naïve, baby Christians, totally ignorant of what they were doing, and so God had mercy on them in their ignorance and continued to develop them after their departure.
2. They were mature Christians but returned after some time to right their wrongs.

There may be other reasons out there, but these were the only two given by our polling group. As a pastor, I can bear witness with these explanations and can think of no other possible scenarios that would permit a successful life after a carnal and sinful church departure.

Attitudes And Communication

No matter why you may be changing churches, there are some very common dos and don'ts every Christian should be familiar with. The two most critical components to leaving a church are *honor* and *communication*.

Honor is a critical character trait that should define every believer, and communication ensures that your exit is not like a soldier's desertion. Because the local church is the crown jewel of the Lord Jesus Christ and the focal point of His work in the earth, leaving it must be done honorably and with clear communication.

If you have truly been serving the church of your departure with a pure heart, chances are you've put down deep roots. If that's the case, you will find leaving your church to be emotionally difficult. This is completely acceptable, and God will be faithful to help you uproot and transplant. On the other hand, if you find leaving your church to be an easy decision and there is no pull on your heart, it may be that either you never put down any roots or, perhaps, what roots you did have began to rot sometime in the past. If this is the case, please be mindful that the next church will not be of much benefit to you.

The Honorable Attitude

As they say, attitude is everything. Honor is an attitude. Honor is not agreement. Honor is not obedience. Honor is an attitude of respect and value we hold toward someone or something. The first commandment with promise is to honor father and mother—not obey—honor. You can honor without obeying, and you can obey without honoring. Honor is commanded numerous times throughout the Bible; most notably for our study is the commandment from Romans 13:7 to show honor where honor is due. Certainly, honor is due toward the local church and its leader, the pastor.

Honor is the most important ingredient when it comes to changing churches. Without it, you'll never land safely. God stated in 1 Samuel 2:30 (CSB), "those who honor me I will honor, but those who despise me will be disgraced." Isaiah 2:2 declares that in the last days the mountain of the Lord's house shall be exalted above all mountains. Among other things, this means that the House of God should be treated with more honor than anything else. You can't honor God by dishonoring a local church or the pastor. Dishonorably leaving one church for another guarantees that disgrace will follow you.

The local church is an extension of the Body of Christ. The pastor is a laborer for God whom believers are commanded to esteem very highly in love for his *work's* sake,[2] not for his doctrine or leadership style. We should have an attitude of honor toward the church and pastor when we leave, even if we believe them to be in error, sin, or heresy. We don't honor the church or the pastor because we agree with them; we honor them because they are both ordained by God. If the church of our departure is in fact in sin or heresy, we can demonstrate honor toward them by interceding fervently for their repentance even after we leave.

If we want God to honor us at our new church, what follows are six acts of honor I believe we should strive for before saying good-bye. These are not set in stone with the finger of God, but as a pastor, if I'm

---

[2] 1 Thessalonians 5:13

sending someone out or receiving a new member, these six actions serve as a powerful testimony of character and integrity. No matter why you may be leaving your current church, these practices will guarantee an honorable departure.

1. Give an honorable explanation to leadership.
2. Give an honorable time notice for your departure.
3. Train up your replacement.
4. Leave a "going away" offering.
5. Ask your pastor to publicly pray for you and send you off.
6. Request a letter of commendation to take with you to your next church.

The Honorable Explanation

As members of the Body of Christ and members one of another, I believe we owe one another explanations for our absences and departures. Only the arrogant man declares, "I don't owe anybody an explanation." Yes, you do. We are members one of another,[3] and we rise and fall on the strengths, weaknesses, victories, and losses of each other. Yes, we do owe one another explanations—not excuses—honest explanations.

Paul described the individual members of the local church as being fitly *framed* together[4] and fitly *joined* together.[5] The first is an allegory of a building; the second is an allusion to the human body. Once a brick is laid in a foundation or a steel beam is bolted in place, they don't get to just up and disappear. The structural integrity of the building is resting upon them. And a human bone or an internal organ doesn't get to just up and disappear overnight. The life and health of that body depends on the consistent function of every body part. So it is with the Body of Christ and its members in particular. We don't get to just up and disappear. God will never permit you to vanish from the local church.

---

[3] Romans 12:5
[4] Ephesians 2:21
[5] Ephesians 4:16

GENERAL DOS AND DON'TS

If you are preparing to leave a local church, you owe an explanation or at least a fair warning to someone in leadership. If you believe God is directing you to move, let the pastor know so he can be praying with you on the matter. If your career or family matters are moving you out of town, let your pastor know so he can pray for you, offer you biblical wisdom, perhaps recommend a good church in that city, or help in other ways. Honest explanations are honorable. Excuses are not.

The Honorable Notice

I have observed that some Christians seem to honor the secular realm of employment and mammon more than they do the sacred realm of the Church and the Kingdom. How so you ask? Simple. They gladly give their employer a two weeks' notice when resigning or changing jobs because it's "the right thing to do," but they won't do the same for their pastor and church family. I don't understand how a Christian can show such honor for a job and such dishonor for the Kingdom, but it happens every day. At the very least, ethical and mannerly church departures should equal the world's culture of a two weeks' notice. This allows for the congregation—our fellow brothers and sisters in Christ whom we claim to love so much—to prepare their hearts for the transition.

An adequate and honorable notice also allows your position in the ministry of helps to be filled, not just abandoned. In the secular realm, the higher ranking you are, the longer it will take to train your replacement; therefore, the greater a notice you would give either before your retirement or before you leave for "greener pastures."

Some believers have no such honor for the local church and walk away with only an email notice (if even that). Some will be a bit more gracious and make an actual phone call. Others might send a text message only after they've left (how magnanimous of them). Still, others just slink out the backdoor without any notice at all. Their dishonorable departure is only discovered through the church grapevine after a chance run-in with the vagabond sheep at the local grocery store. My first pastor used to observe "only rebellious teenagers sneak out the backdoor." How accurate and fitting.

All of these examples demonstrate varying degrees of dishonor, especially for a pastor and a body of believers that were probably once served with and prayed for. A good rule of thumb would be the longer you have served at a local church, the more of a notice you owe them. This is honorable.

I once had a 25-year member and leader in my church resign his membership and position with a letter. He never informed me of his decision or even his intentions face-to-face. The resignation letter was the first I heard of it. Even worse, he sent me the letter when I was out of town. It was his intention to never come back, and he felt that a letter of resignation was sufficient.

Upon my return home, I took his letter to his place of employment, threw it on his desk in righteous anger and said, "You have been a member of our church for 25 years. You have served as an elder, a worship team member, a Sunday school teacher, and my own discipler. You don't get to walk away with a letter. You will come back to our church this Sunday, you will stand in the pulpit, and you will tell *your* church family you love them and give them a face-to-face good-bye."

To his credit, he honored me and obeyed my request. Why wouldn't he? It wasn't an unreasonable request. On the contrary, it was a bare minimum request for honor and maturity. However, he never trained up his replacement—not as an elder, not as a musician, not as a teacher. After serving our church for 25 years, he left to go to another church only a few minutes down the road.

Train Up Your Replacement

If your church and pastor have entrusted you with any kind of leadership position, they have honored you by extending to you a portion of the Gospel burden. Therefore, it is your duty to return the honor by training up your replacement before you leave. This is, of course, contingent upon your pastor's approval. (He may prefer you not train your replacement.) And why wouldn't you want to honor your pastor, your church family, and those under your particular position of leadership?

GENERAL DOS AND DON'TS

I've got to believe that if you've been leading a church department for any length of time, you've probably developed some level of love or affinity for those under you. A loving leader can't help but ensure that their department will carry on with excellence after their departure. It would be extremely selfish and very dishonorable to simply walk away from a church and position without first showing your replacement how to do what you have been doing for the Kingdom. To abandon post like that is to sin against the Lord Jesus Christ by bringing injury to one of His local churches. Don't do it. Make sure your position is cared for.

Leave A "Going Away" Offering

You may not believe it, but Christians often steal from churches when they leave. I'm not kidding! Depending on their position in leadership, they'll steal things like supplies, money, technology, books, address lists, and even people. Don't do that. In fact, do just the opposite. Give on your way out!

Nothing proves the heart quite like money, and no one likes to give money to something they don't believe in. When you're in love, it's easy to give money. When you believe in a cause, it's easy to give money. But when you're offended, the natural tendency is to withdraw the hand of liberality and benevolence. This is why, should you find yourself transitioning from one church to another, giving a "going away" offering is always a good test of your heart's attitude towards the ministry of departure. It's also a good way to thumb your nose at the enemy.

If your heart delights to give the departure offering, honor resides in your soul. If the mere thought of giving some of your money to "that church" vexes your soul and angers your heart, you probably have some attitude adjustments to make.

I recommend giving the church you are leaving a departing gift for several reasons: 1) it will prove your heart and attitude, 2) it will be a blessing to that church and pastor, and 3) it will serve as spiritual warfare against the enemy and any discord he would love to see arise.

Public Prayer

If you are leaving the local church properly and with the right attitude, it would be completely proper for you to ask your pastor to publicly lay hands on you (and your family), praying over you as you are "sent" out to your next kingdom assignment. It has been said, "Some were sent and some just went." To be sent is honorable. To just leave is not.

To be sent is like an official commissioning in the Kingdom of God. This public act will serve as an example and testimony to the rest of the congregation that you (and your family) are, in fact, honorable saints leaving as friends of the church, and that you are not leaving as enemies or opponents. This simple act will glorify Jesus, serve as a public service announcement, and save everyone from a lot of discomfort when you have that inevitable run-in at the local supermarket. This public act also represents the leadership's endorsement of you as their last act of spiritual authority over you before you leave.

Letters Of Commendation

Finally, request a letter of commendation. If you are unfamiliar with this practice, a letter of commendation is a lot like a reference letter from a former employer or professor when you begin job hunting. It's a letter written by your current church leadership recommending you to the new church. In essence, it's a letter vouching for your character and testimony.

Many mainline denominational churches still practice sending and receiving letters of commendation when their congregants transfer church membership. This practice is established in the New Testament. When Apollos wanted to go across from Ephesus to Achaia, the brethren wrote letters to the disciples there exhorting them to receive him.[6]

We see another reference to the common practice of letters of commendation in Paul's second epistle to the Corinthian church. In 2 Corinthians 3:1, due to the negative influence of false ministers, Paul had to

---

[6] See Acts 18:24-28.

defend himself to his own church. He sarcastically asked the hypothetical question, "Are we beginning to commend ourselves again? We don't need letters of recommendation to you or from you as some other people do, do we?"[7] The obvious answer is an overwhelming *no*! No, you don't need a letter of commendation when people know you. You need them when people don't know you. Again, it is clear that letters of recommendation help to vouch for a Christian's character, reputation, and testimony.

The book of Romans begins its final chapter as a letter of recommendation for Sister Phoebe. It states, "I [Paul] commend unto you our sister Phoebe . . . receive her . . . and that you help her in whatever matter she may have need of you; for she herself has also been a helper of many, and of myself as well" (Romans 16:1-2 NASB).

This passage provides a good pattern for modern letters of commendation. The pattern is simple. A letter of commendation could include:

- The name of the person being commended (Sister Phoebe).
- Their reputation (Phoebe was a servant of the church at Cenchrea).
- What the recommendations are concerning the person (receive Phoebe in the Lord and help her in whatever matters she needs).
- A possible reiteration of their reputation (Phoebe has been a helper of many).

What church wouldn't gladly receive and help someone like Sister Phoebe if she presented such a wonderful letter from her previous pastor or elders? If you are leaving your church honorably, it should be very easy to ask for and receive a similar, glowing letter of recommendation.[8]

Review

In summary, here are six things we can do to honor Jesus Christ when we leave a local church:

---

[7] New English Translation
[8] Some pastors may choose to forgo letters of commendation and instead call the new member's previous church to discuss their reputation and obtain a character reference.

1. **Give An Honorable Explanation**. Speak directly with church leadership, preferably face-to-face.
2. **Give An Honorable Time Notice**. Don't honor pharaoh and mammon with a two weeks' notice without extending at least the same honor to the local church.
3. **Train up your replacements.** If you are in position(s) of leadership, you owe it to your pastor and the rest of the local church to train up your replacement(s).
4. **Leave a "going away" offering.** Nothing proves the heart quite like money. If you are leaving your church right, it will be easy to give one final offering.
5. **Have your pastor publicly pray for you.** As a testimony to the rest of the saints, it is honorable to ask your pastor and/or presbytery to pray for you (and your family) as you depart from your current church and are reconnected to a new local church.
6. **Request a letter of commendation.** This is easy, honorable, biblical, and it goes a long way in helping you, the believer, to establish yourself at the new church.

General Don'ts

Below are four things to *never* do when leaving a church. I've personally experienced all four of these unethical practices as people have left our church. The following are absolutely no way to ever treat the Body of Christ! Never:

1. **Just disappear.** This is very selfish and immature, not to mention unprofessional. Don't do it! Demas disappeared on Paul. Paul called it being forsaken. Don't forsake your church. Every pastor I know has experienced this.
2. **Steal on the way out.** Often people will steal on the way out the door from their church. They'll steal supplies, address lists, or even people. Don't do it! Judas stole from Jesus. He will forever

be known as a traitor and a thief. Every pastor I know has experienced this.
3. **Slander/Gossip.** Depending on why you left your church, it might be tempting to run them down. Don't do it! Absalom slandered his father, King David, in an attempt to overthrow him. God defended David and allowed Absalom to die tragically. Every pastor I know has experienced this.
4. **Leave Bitter.** Bitterness is a root that can only produce bitter fruit everywhere you go. The Bible warns that a bitter heart will make trouble for you and defile the people around you.[9] Don't do it. Don't leave bitter.

How you leave your current church will make all the difference in your personal testimony. Don't be a Demas, a Judas, or an Absalom. Aim to be an Elisha who was faithful until the very end. Be like Luke, who never departed Paul's side. Look to be a Timothy who was sent out by Paul and then recalled by Paul when he needed help. The Church is not to run like the world. The Church has been given the Kingdom's culture. We should live like it.

What To Do If You've Left Wrong

The short answer is repent! "To repent" doesn't mean you necessarily need to go back, but you can't possibly expect God to bless your future endeavors leaving a church with a lousy attitude, bitterness, gossip, slander, or unforgiveness in your heart. I would strongly recommend that anyone guilty of dishonorably leaving a previous church humble themselves, make a simple phone call, and repent to their former pastor. Most pastors I know would graciously accept the apology and do whatever was necessary to help their former member to advance in life.

Depending on how sinful the departure was, other actions may be appropriate, e.g., return or recompense stolen items, publish a social media

---

[9] Hebrews 12:15

apology repenting of any slander or gossip posted on the same platform, or maybe personally make amends with anyone you have hurt. True repentance will jump through absolutely any hoop or hurdle to make things right. As John the Baptist preached, the key is to, "prove by the way you live that you have repented of your sins and turned to God."[10]

As stated in the introduction, there are six main reasons why Christians leave their local church. Each of the next six chapters will delve into those particular reasons and also offer a "parachute" of wisdom for how to land safely at the next church. I will assume the reader understands what a parachute is and how it is used to provide a safe and soft landing upon exiting an aircraft.

---

[10] Matthew 3:8 NLT

PART TWO

The Six Parachutes Of Church Departure

6
THE "DIVINE REASSIGNMENT" PARACHUTE

The first reason Christians will leave their current church is because God has divinely reassigned them elsewhere. We'll define a *divine reassignment* as God transferring you from your current location and role in the Kingdom to another location and role in the Kingdom. The critical point to keep in mind is that a divine reassignment will always involve some activity that further advances the Kingdom, improves your walk with Jesus, and glorifies God. A divine reassignment is a promotion, not a demotion. This makes it the most biblical reason for a Christian to leave a church.

Divine reassignments cover a wide range of possibilities. They can include sending a missionary out to their mission post or sending a young 18-year-old off to military boot camp. Moving your family across the country to help a pastor start a new church would definitely be a reassignment. Other divine reassignments can include a call to seminary, college, or Bible school. Each of these examples would require a Christian to leave their local church in order to obey God. As previously stated, it is assumed your reassignment involves some form of activity that further advances the Kingdom, improves your walk with Jesus, and glorifies God. We see these three criteria fulfilled in the aforementioned missionary assignments, seminary or Bible school enrollments, church planting endeavors, and even divine calls to military service.

A divine reassignment won't happen on a whim, in the heat of an offensive sermon, when you're being rebuked in your pastor's office, or in the middle of a disagreement with a fellow nursery worker. At the very least, a divine reassignment is usually months in the works. In fact, it has been my experience that the longer you have faithfully served a local church, the more of a notice the Holy Spirit will give you before moving you on to the next assignment. This is because God will never promote you at the expense of His servants.

A divine reassignment will very rarely send you to a new church five minutes away, unless, of course, the new church would be a spiritual step up in doctrine, holiness, consecration, and righteousness. God never reassigns His children to a lesser church, and by lesser church I mean a church of lower biblical standards. That would be a demotion. Our God is always calling us upward in Him, not downward to an easier church (more on that in Chapter 10).

When a Christian believes they are being divinely reassigned to a new church (or ministry), many emotions will arise. Excitement, fear, joy, sorrow, dread, anticipation, etc. Excitement for the next phase of Christian service, but fear of the unknown and how to walk it out. Joy over the promotion of God, yet sorrow over leaving a beautiful church family. Dread over all the forthcoming changes, but anticipation to see what new thing God is wanting to do. A divine reassignment can truly be an emotional rollercoaster—and that's okay!

How To Walk Out A Reassignment

If you perceive God is reassigning you, it will bear witness with leadership and the core group of believers at your church. If no one feels good about your move, it may be time to fall back and pray some more. If you are unwilling to hear objections from those who love you, it may be time to ask, "Why am I so eager to get out of here?" I've never really understood why some Christians are so eager to leave a strong, healthy church, but some people are just incapable of being content.

Don't expect God to treat a New Testament Christian's reassignment like He did Abraham's departure from Ur. He will never tell a believer, "Leave your local church for a new church that you know not of, and I will reveal it to you when you arrive there." I have had too many precious saints, perfectly safe and well-fed in our church, decide they needed to go find a new church for no real reason. Several have said just what I have mocked, "God is leading us to go visit other churches." Really? Any idea why? They never seemed to have a sound biblical answer, but they "must obey God." Funny, that drive to sacrifice and "obey God" was never very strong while they were at my church, but at the first inclination to depart, they suddenly found the faith to overcome the obstacles of inconvenience.

A gentleman from our congregation once came to me and said, "Pastor, God is leading us to leave your church and attend this church over here." This notion did not bear witness with me whatsoever and made absolutely no sense for several reasons: 1) this came out of nowhere, 2) we were in the middle of a remodeling project and God doesn't reassign Nehemiah's help in the middle of wall building, 3) the other church was literally just minutes away, 4) the other church was very lukewarm, and 5) this family had been with our church in leadership for over 20 years.

In an attempt to help the husband walk out this "leading," I encouraged him to visit the other church on occasion, "spy out the land," and see what God might say to him or his wife while they were there. He admitted they had already been visiting the other church a little. I then asked him to wait until the end of our three-month long remodeling project before making a decision. This would give him more time to pray about it and help maintain the morale of our church in the midst of our project. He graciously honored me and agreed to do so.

Ironically, a few weeks later he came to me and said, "Well, Pastor, I was wrong. That church over there isn't where God wants us to go." I asked what made him change his mind. He said that the usher assigned to his section had reeked of alcohol two Sundays in a row and that God would definitely not have him leave our church for a drinking church. For a moment I rejoiced, convinced he was going to settle back down in our church—the church he had raised his family in for over 20 years. My joy was short-lived. He then said, "Now I think God is wanting us to go to this church over there ("over there" being my friend's church a few minutes away in a different direction)."

Once again, I tried to gently help him test his leading. None of it made any sense, nor did it feel right to me. In the end, he and his family left honorably and respectfully. We prayed for them and sent them 10 minutes away to the other church. When they arrived, my friend called me and asked, "What in the world is this family doing at my church?" To which I replied, "I haven't got a clue. I tried to help them walk this out. But they're good people. Just a little confused right now. They won't give you any problems."

My friend received them and pastored them as best he could, but their lives soon began to fall apart. Rebellion, sexual sin, and a premature death ravaged the precious family's lives. Because neither I nor my pastor friend believed their reassignment was the will of God, my heart can't help but wonder what their destiny might have looked like if they had simply stayed put.

On another occasion, I was called upon to help a young adult church member still living at home with her parents. The mother brought to me her concerns about her adult daughter. The young lady had been staying out late and returning smelling like cigarette smoke. As to be expected, the mother was angry, frustrated, and distressed about her daughter's extremely irresponsible and carnal behavior. I met with the young lady to try and figure out what was going on.

During our discussion it came to light that she was sleeping around. I chastised her concerning these reckless decisions and the disregard for her Christian walk. She left my office apologetic and broken but reassured in the fact that I loved her and that I only wanted the best for her and her future.

Amazingly, three days later she called to tell me God had spoken to her to leave our church and go to another church a few minutes away. She left slandering us. The poor girl didn't stay very long at the other church either before she totally backslid into a heinous life of perversion. How sad and completely preventable. This was definitely not a divine reassignment.

On the other hand, I have seen families genuinely reassigned by God leave our church properly and flourish in life. We've successfully sent out many singles and families to go serve at other churches or help other ministries, pursue a college career, attend Bible college, move overseas for world missions, or even serve in the military. Praise God! They honored God, and we were able to send them out properly with His blessing!

The "Divine Reassignment" Parachute

So you believe God is supernaturally reassigning you to another church? Here are several things you can do to walk this season out. This isn't necessarily a list of hard-fast rules, but if the heart behind each one is followed, they will serve to greatly improve your success in your endeavor.

Submit your plans to leadership. Your pastor has been anointed by God to watch over your soul.[1] If we look to the natural allegory of sheep and shepherds, shepherds stand three to four feet taller than sheep and can see a lot further off. God's shepherds are the same way; they can see things sheep can't. Furthermore, pastors are experts at all things "church." There is no doubt your pastor will have insight and wisdom concerning the changes you may be facing.

Many years ago, when I was a young geologist and youth leader, God spoke to me to move from Tennessee to the Midwest in order to attend Bible school. I quickly submitted the notion of moving out of state for Bible school to my pastor and my spiritual father (both were in different cities). This was to be the largest change I had ever made, and I desperately needed their input. If it bore witness with them that it was the will of God,

---

[1] Hebrews 13:17

I wanted their wisdom to walk it out. But if they didn't feel good about it, I wanted to know ASAP so I could pull the plug on it altogether.

Man's heart is quite fickle and the Bible is clear; our hearts can fabricate plans and then pass them off as divine.[2] Submitting those plans to leadership can help you distinguish between what the Spirit of God has said and what a deceitful heart has vainly imagined. The difference between the two can be very difficult to distinguish.

Take your time and proceed with caution. Proverbs 19:2 (NLT) declares, "haste makes mistakes." Proverbs 2:11 says, "Discretion shall preserve thee, . . ." Hear what the wisdom of God says: don't get in a hurry! The bigger the move God is requiring of you, the more time He will give you. This is only fair and reasonable—just like our God!

With my move to Bible school I had to change states, churches, jobs, life direction, and find a replacement youth leader—all of which could not be done honorably with a month's notice. About four months before my date of departure, I actually took a trip to the new city to "spy out the land." While there, I interviewed for a job, visited a church, and looked around for a place to live. The whole trip was also meant to be a way to cautiously feel out the move and see if I still retained the peace of God while I was there or if I was pursuing an imagination of my heart. In the end, it proved to be the will of God, and from the time God spoke to me until the day I moved to Bible school was almost exactly one year.

More recently, our former youth leaders were on a youth mission trip to Honduras when God called them to be missionaries. The husband perceived that this calling would soon come to pass. But from the time they received that call to world missions until the day they moved to East Africa to be full-time missionaries was almost two years. Moving from Tennessee to East Africa is a big reassignment. It took two years for them to get everything in order and to honorably make the transition. A good rule of thumb is: the bigger the move, the more time God will give you to get your house in order and make the move.

---

[2] See Proverbs 16:1, 9; 19:21; Jeremiah 17:9.

Pray. Any divine move will require prayer, prayer, and more prayer. Before Ezra moved a remnant of Jews from Persia back to Jerusalem, he took several days to pray, fast, and seek God.[3] This was in spite of the fact that his move was the sure will of God and he had King Artaxerxes' support.

Ezra prayed for a safe journey for the adults, the children, and all their substance. God was intreated of them, and their long journey[4] was completely uneventful (those are the best kind of long journeys). As the New Living Translation summarizes it, "And the gracious hand of our God protected us and saved us from enemies and bandits along the way" (Ezra 8:31).

Whether you are changing churches, going off to the military or college, being sent out to start a church, or moving overseas to be a missionary, each and every step will require prayer and the help of God. Take your time and seek God for each step of the transition. This is a new season for you, and new seasons can require different, unforeseen disciplines.

Be willing to reverse course if proven wrong. No one's perfect. I think we've all genuinely believed that we had the direction of the Lord only to discover—nope—it wasn't God at all. We must be willing and mature enough to fall back to the last place we knew we were in the will of God. In Joshua's day, they went out and came back to Gilgal. Peter and John went out and always came back to the Jerusalem church. Paul always found refuge at the Antioch church. Be humble enough to admit when you've missed it, and fall back to where you know for sure you were last in the will of God.

I have a family in my church who once moved halfway across the country for a new job, believing it was the will of God. Upon arrival in their new city, they knew instantly by the total lack of peace that they were out of the will of God. The husband quickly called his former boss, apologized, and immediately received his old job back. He then went to his

---

[3] Ezra 8:21
[4] The 900-mile journey from Babylon to Jerusalem took four months.

first day of work and explained to his new boss, "I'm sorry, but this is not going to work." To which the new boss replied, "Really? Seriously? Well, then . . . go home." The couple then reloaded their car and turned around and drove back to where they had moved from. They only spent two days in that new city before moving back. Thank God for their humility and willingness to turn around.

In 2005, I was about to move to Asia to be a missionary. I was being sent by a ministry and received by another ministry. (This is the best way to make a divine transition—there should be a sending team and a receiving team.) Everything was lining up like clockwork. Financial support was coming in and everything was being tidied up Stateside. I sold almost all my possessions and was Asia-bound.

I was in the Detroit airport with all of my earthly possessions in one very large L.L. Bean duffel bag in the cargo hold of a Boeing 747, watching my international flight begin to board when I suddenly became overwhelmed with an intense void of peace. This was not a panic attack. I was not afraid of moving overseas or leaving America. On the contrary, I had been marching toward fulfilling the dream of being a missionary for the previous 10 years of my life. No, this was a peace vacuum. Isaiah 55:12 states that we shall "be led forth with peace." There was absolutely none that day, and the line to board my flight for Asia was getting shorter.

I quickly called my father in the faith to seek his wisdom. Unfortunately, I didn't know then what I know now and hadn't really submitted these major plans to him, though my parents had both discouraged me from my endeavor. They didn't have peace about the move either. My spiritual father encouraged me to be led by the Holy Spirit, which, for me in that moment, meant returning to the last place I had peace. I hung up the phone, cancelled my Asia flight, rebooked a flight home for Tennessee, experienced a very thoroughly invasive private security inspection, and was back in my spiritual father's church that Sunday.

I returned to Tennessee with plenty of shame, a big mess to clean up, tons of apologizing to do, offerings to return, and lots of questions rolling through my head. Questions like: "How did I get so far down the wrong road before realizing I was missing the will of God?" and "Will I ever get overseas?" But at least I was not in Asia. And more importantly, I had the peace of God again. All the other things would slowly take care of themselves.

I learned that there is no shame in making a mistake, especially if it's made with a good heart. The only real shame is in pridefully marching on to your own harm or loss after realizing you're wrong.

If you step out in pursuit of God and find yourself in a waste-howling wilderness of no peace, the best thing you can do is quickly return to the last place you had peace. Do not delay. Do not forge ahead. Don't force a square peg into a round hole. Return to that last place of peace and regather yourself.

A Brief Review

Below are the four critical steps to take when you are walking out a divine reassignment.

1. Submit your plans to leadership.
2. Take your time and proceed with caution.
3. Pray, pray, pray.
4. Be willing to reverse course if proven wrong.

Be of good cheer! God wants to get you where He wants you more than you do. He will order your footsteps.

7
THE "FLEEING APOSTASY" PARACHUTE

As humanity winds down and the Lord's return approaches, many churches and even whole denominations are rapidly corrupting and defecting from the Way of truth. These groups are fulfilling the prophecy of the last days' apostasy.[1] This brings us to the second reason why a Christian might change churches: *to flee apostasy*. Apostasy, heresy, and ecclesiastical corruption are pernicious. As a result, many Christians, in their fidelity to the Holy Scriptures and allegiance to Jesus Christ, are exiting congregations in search of wholesome doctrine and true shepherds. They understand that whoever shepherds your soul guides your faith.

However, many of these believers are reluctant to leave the church or denomination of their childhood. And who can blame them? They have invested years of service, raised their children there, given great sums of tithes and offerings, and maybe even helped to literally build the church.

Perhaps, like Lot's wife looking back at Sodom, their thoughts and memories are on the "good ole days" and not on the present wickedness. But it is precisely because of the "good ole days" that they often have

---

[1] See 1 Timothy 4:1 and 2 Thessalonians 2:3.

trouble reading the writing on the wall as it clearly says *Ichabod—The glory of God has departed.*

Some have even stayed longer than they should, hoping they could make a difference or help turn the ship aright. Their fond memories of past revivals, salvations, and moves of God contend with their church's current atmosphere of heresy, apostasy, and compromise. Though these believers have good intentions, their church may be a hopeless cause.

Eventually these precious saints will find themselves having to flee their beloved church like Lot or like an evacuee in the face of an impending hurricane or unquenchable wildfire. Such believers are changing churches in order to stay faithful to Jesus Christ and finish their course.

Boiling Frogs, Deceived Saints

Much like the often-referenced "boiling frog" analogy, members of apostate churches are often slowly and subtly contaminated by the heretical direction of leadership. If you're unfamiliar with the boiling frog analogy, basically, if you drop a frog in a pot of boiling water, it will instantly jump out in order to preserve itself (naturally). But if you place the same frog in a pot of room-temperature water and then slowly bring the water to a boil, you can effectively kill and cook the frog without the frog ever protesting.

When a church led by a heretic apostatizes, it rarely happens overnight. The church and its congregation members are slowly exposed to heresy and doctrines of devils a little bit at a time, sometimes over many years. This is like bringing the frog to a slow boil. By the time the heresy has been fully taught and dispersed, the minds and souls of the church members are in total sync with the perverse teachings, and they find nothing to protest. The doctrines of devils have now become their prized teachings and pride-filled revelations.

Any church member that has stuck around to the full culmination of heresy will have great difficulty seeing a reason to leave. Their heart and mind will have slowly learned the rhythm of the new "gospel." At this point, it may take divine intervention to get them out of their apostate church, much like Lot had to have an angelic visitation and commandment to leave Sodom. And even then, Lot had to be dragged away by the angels.[2]

Not all heresy looks the same. Heresy can be *passive*, *extra-biblical*, or just outright *antiorthodoxical*. Passive heresy doesn't outright deny any foundational Bible doctrines; it just chooses to omit or ignore them for various reasons, usually due to cowardice or man-pleasing. Extra-biblical heresy also doesn't often deny any traditional Christian orthodoxy. It just tends to get "out there" beyond the Bible. This too is dangerous. The final type of heresy is our good old-fashioned heresy of the blasphemous flavor. This usually includes some form of Christ-denial. Regardless of the heresy you may experience, apostate churches must be abandoned.

A Deceptive New Pastor

I once helped a family member walk through his church's season of *passive heresy*. When their church's greatest pastor retired, the hiring committee quickly went to work to replace him with someone of like, holy faith. Unfortunately, they somehow managed to land a dud. And not just a dud, a near heretic of a dud.

The new pastor began to quickly water down the Gospel and intentionally omit vital Bible truths. Expository Bible teaching was replaced with ear-tickling sermons that failed to train, correct, or even rebuke. Members complained of no longer being taught the meat of the Word. The pastor quit giving altar calls, quit preaching against sin, quit teaching honor for the things of God, and abandoned many other orthodoxically sound practices this church had historically embraced to their own great promotion by God.

In short, the church was quickly becoming seeker-friendly—something they did not want to become. The result: the massive church began to bleed older, longtime families. While new, younger families joined, the net church attendance plummeted. Financial giving plummeted. Grumbling arose. A hundred-year-old church, known for righteousness,

---

[2] Genesis 19:16

salvations, and world missions began to completely break down in less than three years.

My family member was beside himself and rightly so. We had regular phone calls about what could be done. I advised him to be honorable and respectful of the new pastor because he was still, after all, the head of the church. I cautioned him not to unintentionally (or intentionally) become a Korah and rise up against the new pastor, no matter how off-track the church was becoming.

At one point, my family member had a respectful meeting with the new pastor where he tactfully voiced his concerns—to no avail. He finally came to the realization that, in order to stay faithful to the Lord Jesus Christ and the Gospel, he and his wife might have to leave that church. This was an excruciating decision for them because of their years of commitment, but it was one they were willing to make to continue serving God faithfully.

In the end, the boards and committees of their church came together and respectfully asked the new pastor to make some changes to his leadership style and to the content of his sermons. Everything requested was very reasonable and bare-minimum. The new pastor, unwilling to align with the scriptures, resigned within a few days. He was unwilling to adjust his course and pastor the church in accordance with the Bible.

The church went on to find a real pastor after God's own heart and has since flourished again.

Weird Charismatic Shenanigans

I once received a precious family from a charismatic church in another city that had gone a little squirrely (which honestly happens too often in charismatic churches). As usual, the church's goofiness didn't happen overnight. And this family loved their charismatic church . . . at first.

The first problem that arose was the pastor's heavy-handed promotion of a multi-level marketing business. It was said from the pulpit, "We believe in this product, you don't have to be a part of it if you don't want to, but if you trust us, why wouldn't you get in on it?" This is a clear abuse of pastoral trust and, truthfully, not too far from being raw greed. Unfortunately, the pastor abused his congregation's trust and manipulated them to spend money they probably wouldn't have otherwise spent.

The husband told me that when this happened, he said in his heart, "Ok, I can see you're not my pastor, and you don't really care about my family. You're just a preacher that's interested in money." To protect themselves, the family felt like they had to pull back and put up a guard around their heart.

The real deal breaker came when the pastor started talking to angels on a regular basis. And not just talking to angels, but actually getting his sermons from angels. If you didn't know, this is a direct violation of Scripture and can be considered *extra-biblical heresy*.

Though the Bible records angels bringing messages from God, there is absolutely zero precedent of them telling a minister what to preach. The reason angels don't preach the Gospel or teach theology is because they don't understand it. It is still a mystery they are trying to look into.[3] In fact, Paul taught that the mystery of the Gospel had just in his day been revealed to the holy apostles and prophets.[4] He continued in Ephesians 3:10 (NASB) saying that this was so "the manifold wisdom of God might be made known through the church to the rulers and authorities in the heavenly places." In essence, the church is to teach the angelic and demonic spirit realm, not vice versa.

Furthermore, when angels finally do get the chance to preach the Gospel, it's not until the 14th chapter of the Revelation, near the end of the Tribulation period. So, for a pastor to declare that an angel was giving him the message to preach, well, you can understand why this dear family felt like they had no choice but to leave their church.

While writing this book, I revisited this event with the husband just to refresh the details. He stated, "We probably didn't leave as honorably as possible, and we probably didn't do everything right, but there was just no way we could have stayed there. It was miserable. And when we did

---

[3] 1 Peter 1:12
[4] Ephesians 3:5. See also Galatians 1:8.

submit our intentions to leave, the pastor began to actively resist us." That's so sad to hear. The local church should be a place of peace and growth, not internal tension, eggshell-walking, or psychological games.

Old-Fashioned Heresy

A friend of mine encountered the third type of heresy: classic old-fashioned *antiorthodoxy*. After moving to a different state, my friend and his wife found a long-established, Bible-believing church in which to plant themselves. Things started off fine enough for the first few years as they got deeply involved in serving.

About the fourth year they were there, the pastor made a statement while preaching that caught my friend's ear. He declared, "Jesus came to destroy the very idea of law." Though such a statement might be doctrinally permissible to say with a few caveats and explanations, it still flirts dangerously close with lawlessness and antinomianism.[5] Unfortunately, this was not the case as the pastor did not correct or give a suitable context for his statement. In fact, the notion of Christians not being accountable or responsible to any form of law or Kingdom rules became the theme of most sermons for several years. Over time, the doctrinal flirtation with lawlessness slowly turned to the subtle notion that Jesus Christ was not divine.

From this time forward, most of the pastor's sermons were spent emphasizing the humanity of Jesus and that everything He did, He did as a man. Though the pastor would never vocally deny the deity of Christ, never teaching the divinity of Jesus can very quickly become the same thing.

Heresy usually begins as an overemphasis of a single Bible truth. The best way to avoid the slippery slope of unintentional heresy is to be like Paul and teach the whole counsel of God.[6] In this case, that would

---

[5] The heresy that states Christians are free from the moral law of God's Word due to grace. Jude 4 calls this practice "turning the grace of God into lasciviousness."
[6] Acts 20:27

have included teaching on the divinity of Jesus. One of Christianity's foundational doctrines is the mystery of Jesus Christ being fully God and fully man. Denying the hypostatic union of Jesus Christ is an ancient heresy called Nestorianism.[7]

It might be hard to imagine that a conservative, evangelical Bible-teaching church could end up espousing such an ancient heresy, but that's exactly what happened. And it didn't happen overnight. From the time of the first doctrinal swerve until my friend realized he had to flee was eight years. My friend related to me that he knew it was time to leave when he and his wife became more concerned with sending their son to Sunday school than they were with sending him to public school.

Even more disconcerting is the fact that the pastor was no inexperienced baby preacher. After over 30 years of ministry, his doctrinal drift began when he was in his 60s. Thankfully, my friend was a well-trained and devout student of God's Word, so his pastor's doctrinal drift did not go unnoticed. Unfortunately, many were not as astute and remained in the church. The damage of this heresy was observed months later when someone still at the church randomly asked, "Does it even matter if Jesus was God?" Yes, it does. Our entire salvation depends upon it!

Vomited Up

There may be the rare occasion where a church and/or its leadership slowly turns dirty and compromised without the congregation members knowing it. I have witnessed this on a few occasions, perhaps less than five times. When this kind of covert corruption takes place, more than likely, the righteous, holy believer will usually end up being run out, expelled, or "vomited up." When darkness is in the leadership, light will be expelled.

When King Saul turned evil, David was chased away time and again. Please don't fall into the common delusion of thinking that you can stay

---

[7] Named for Nestorius, the 5th Century Patriarch of Constantinople whose teachings subtly denied that Jesus Christ contained two natures in one divine person, a.k.a. the unity of subsistence or hypostasis. His doctrine overemphasized the humanity of Christ.

in a corrupt church and help turn it. Or the other common deception I've often heard, "But if I go, who will be there to help the people who still want God?" That's not your problem. David couldn't steer Israel until he was officially made king. You will never be able to steer or fix a church you don't pastor.

The "Fleeing Apostasy" Parachute

So, what can a Christian do? How do we escape the deception of a church that is slowly corrupting?

First and foremost, we must make every effort to walk with God outside of our regular church attendance. This includes being a student of the Word and a person of prayer. In fact, be an *avid* student of God's Word. Be as the noble Bereans that refused to blindly follow even the great Apostle Paul. They went home and searched the scriptures to see if Paul was accurate. God's Word is truth, and it will vaccinate us against heresy, false teachings, and lying pulpits.

Be a person of daily prayer. Prayer (as well as worship) is how we get to know God's presence. Prayer gives the Spirit of Truth the opportunity to speak to us. When we are familiar with the presence of God, we'll be able to recognize when a church or a minister begins to veer off course. I can tell you firsthand as a pastor, ministers can grieve the Holy Spirit while we stand in the pulpit. If you, as a layperson are sensitive to the Holy Spirit, you'll be able to perceive His grief when a preacher violates the Word or the will of God.

Also, realize that our allegiance isn't to a pastor, a church, or even a denomination; our allegiance is to Jesus Christ. Being a member of a church doesn't obtain eternal life for us. Being a member of the Body of Christ through the new birth is the only membership critical for eternal life.

Should you ever find yourself in the horrible position of having to leave a church to flee apostasy, I still recommend following as many of the six *dos* from Chapter 5 as possible. It's hard to go wrong being honorable.

Remember how David repeatedly honored King Saul? It seems the more lunatic and murderous Saul became, the more honor David exhibited. The paranoid King Saul was determined to hunt down David and murder him for no justifiable reason. On two occasions David had the opportunity to kill him and be free from the torment of pursuit, but in both instances he chose to honor the king.[8] I believe the honor shown by David wasn't just because it was the proper thing to do, but also because David fondly remembered the "good ole days" when his beloved king was in a much better place spiritually. The honor David showed Saul served to promote the young king for many years.

When leaving an apostate church, I believe the *honorable explanation* is the most important action. This of course will require you to be honest about why you are really leaving. If the pastor will meet with you, an honest and respectful explanation allows the pastor to hear your concerns about heresy and the direction of the church. I know personally, if I had several families leave my church and they were all brave enough to respectfully voice the same concern, I would have no choice but to judge myself and hopefully make some necessary adjustments. God intends to use your departure to get the pastor's attention. Understand that your departure is a form of divine judgment against that church and pastor. When God smites a shepherd, the sheep will flee.[9]

The other five recommendations (*give an honorable time notice, train up your replacement, leave a "going away" offering, request public prayer,* and *request a letter of commendation*) should be followed as much as possible, though depending on the nature of the heresy or apostasy, some may not be very practical.

Do refrain from gossip and slander. And certainly, if you love the pastor and the church family, and you should, continue to pray for their

---

[8] In 1 Samuel 24, David had the opportunity to kill King Saul in a cave. Rather than kill him, David cut off a swatch of the king's robe. In 1 Samuel 26, David, accompanied by Abishai, entered into King Saul's camp near Jeshimon while he slept. Rather than murder the king, David stole his spear and jug of water.
[9] Zechariah 13:7

repentance and preservation. The key is to be honorable as you depart so that God can honor you at your new church.

8
THE "I'M HUNGRIER FOR MORE OF GOD" PARACHUTE

The third reason Christians leave their current church is due to spiritual hunger. Not all Christians are equal. Not all Christians desire God with the same fervency. There has always been and will always be a spectrum of Christian hunger, from the ice-cold backslider to the hot, on-fire, soul-winning prayer warrior. Some believers are just *hungry for more of God* even when everyone around them is not.

It is this hunger for better teaching, better worship, and more of the presence of the Holy Spirit that causes them to sit restless in their current church. It is their hunger for change, hunger for deliverance and freedom, and hunger to see God move in a mighty way that causes their heart to long for green pastures and still waters. Their heart for God is simply not satisfied with the level of Christianity being offered at their current church.

They may genuinely love their pastor and their church family, but they crave more of the divine. They happily follow their pastor, but he just isn't leading them deep enough. And truly, a congregation will only be able to go as deep or as far as the leadership permits. If the shepherd is less than spiritual, less than holy, less than knowledgeable about God's Word, spiritual starvation is all but inevitable.

Reasons for newfound spiritual hunger pangs can vary, but two are more pronounced than any other: 1) a divine awakening in an individual or 2) an unbiblical change in church direction.

A personal awakening implies that the believer has been asleep. Once awakened to the reality of the Kingdom, the moving of the Spirit, and the richness of the Word, hanging around sleepy Christians is going to be tremendously frustrating. An awakened Christian will usually only be satisfied in their current church until they have gobbled up everything the pastor and the ministry have to offer, at which time they will either need to move on to continue to grow or remain there and enter a spiritual plateau. At some point spiritual plateaus recede back into spiritual slumber. It's a cycle I believe the enemy enjoys watching.

The second scenario that sends Christians in search of a "better" church (that of an unbiblical change in church direction) is out of the believer's control and can be painfully frustrating. I can't imagine being a part of a church I love and watching leadership steer the church away from God and into secular methods. These directional changes are typically seismic in magnitude and leave church members longing for more of what drew them to that church in the first place.

A Personal Awakening

There are countless Christians who have been faithful to a church for a long time, usually attending because it's all they know and it's comfortable. They fall into the routine of regular attendance, service, and giving. They know the church's culture, songs, liturgy, and formality by heart. By every practical measure, we'd probably categorize them as either devoutly religious or just sleepwalking through their Christianity.

Then something amazing happens. They have an encounter with God and their world is turned upside-down. Maybe it was a chance encounter with a guest minister. Maybe a special Bible study. Maybe they were invited to a friend's church. Maybe tragedy struck close to home causing them to press into God deeper than ever before. Or, perhaps just a tough season of life struck and as Job indicated, "He gets their attention through adversity" (Job 36:15 NLT).

Regardless, they have been set on fire by God, and the current church environment may not be enough to satisfy their newly lit flame. For this reason, they must seek out a place that can give them more of God.

Seeker-Friendly Starvation

The most glaring example of spiritual starvation is the huge popularity of the seeker-friendly movement. This church growth philosophy has swept through the American church like a wildfire. Churches of every size, caliber, and almost every denomination have embraced it. So widespread and enduring has been this church trend, the ill-informed might have actually mistaken it for a genuine revival. However, when one examines the fruit produced by this movement, it becomes painfully evident that "seeker" churches look more like a falling away from God than a real Spirit-breathed revival. Holy Spirit revivals clean people up and set people on fire. The seeker-friendly movement has taught believers to lower biblical standards and chill out in their zeal.

Just consider some of the stereotypical aspects of the average church that has embraced the wildly popular seeker-friendly philosophy:

- **Motivational/self-help messages.** This style of message has been borrowed from the secular world. Real preachers preach the Gospel and real teachers teach sound doctrine. Real pastors are faithful to Jesus Christ. "They will lead you with knowledge and insight" (Jeremiah 3:15b NET).
- **Shorter sermons.** The argument for this compromise is that modern Christians no longer have the attention span and you'll lose their interest, never mind the fact that they easily watch three-hour ballgames on Saturdays. This symptom is a partial fulfillment of 2 Timothy 4:3: "they will not endure sound doctrine." As one old-timey preacher told me, "Sermonettes produce Christianettes."

- **Fewer church services.** Gone is the Sunday school hour that preceded the Sunday morning service. Also long gone is the Sunday evening service. The mid-week service is all but extinct, too. Are you keeping track so far? This means that the only church service the average seeker-friendly ministry is offering is one shortened service a week, and that message is likely to be filled with pop-psychology and self-help mumbo-jumbo. Where is the meat of God's Word? What is often offered cannot even rightly be classified as milk. It's condensed milk. So condensed in fact, it's almost caramel. Christians need more church, not less.
- **No altar calls.** Even if you don't call it an altar call, there should be time given to respond to the message delivered, assuming the message had some kind of call to action or repentance. Seeker churches have abolished the traditional altar call because they make people uncomfortable. In fact, seeker churches often abolish biblical words like *sin, repent, hell, judgment,* and *damnation.* Why? Because these words are described as "uncomfortable."
- **The absence of prayer services.** We can't forget that Jesus, quoting Isaiah 56:7, declared that the House of God must be a house of prayer. A senior pastor/missionary once explained to me, "Sunday morning attendance shows you the church is popular. Sunday night attendance shows you the preacher is popular. Wednesday night attendance shows you the message is popular. But your prayer service attendance, well, that shows you who God is popular with."
- **The lack of discipleship.** Since discipleship requires confrontation, discipline, and change, it shouldn't surprise us that discipleship is also usually absent from a seeker-friendly church. If discipleship has always been the second part of the Great Commission, then why is it being neglected?
- **Carnal worship.** Music styles change, but the standard for worship lyrics and presentation mustn't. Much of modern worship looks and sounds no different than a grunge band playing at a local

coffee house on a Friday night. I personally believe King David, the greatest of all Bible worshipers, would have had many of today's worship leaders cut asunder for their lack of respect and reverence for the Holy One of Israel.

- **Gimmicks.** In the race to Americanize the Church and market its services to the local community, church leaders often resort to gimmicks and carnival-like attractions. Other than the quintessential American foyer coffee bar, modern gimmicks can include movie-themed sermon series, t-shirt cannons, buffalo-wing eating contests (and other pre-service "ice-breakers"), game nights, hosting entertainers in place of Gospel ministers, etc. The point is, they harness the power of the American culture to draw people, and by doing so they seem to forget the promise Jesus Christ made: "And if I be lifted up, I will draw all men unto me." One hero of the faith observed, "You can't preach the world to the world to win the world!" What's the point of chasing all of America's entertaining accoutrements? They've never ushered in the presence of God.

After reading this bulleted list, we must ask ourselves what caliber of Christian is really being produced at a church like this? I don't think anyone would be naïve enough to truly think this is what Jesus had in mind when He hung on the Cross. Nor is it a picture of what the apostles gave their lives for. Can you imagine what the Apostle Paul would say if, while visiting the church of Ephesus, the local pastor warmed up the crowd by shooting church logo t-shirts out of a cannon?

Not surprisingly, this style of ministry has been rather adept at growing large churches, but it has failed to disciple strong saints. When did we begin to think that numbers were the biblical metric for success? Jesus never commended any of the seven churches of the Revelation for their Sunday morning attendance. In fact, we have no idea how large or small those early churches were. What we do know is that the largest, richest church of the seven—Laodicea—was close to being vomited out of the Kingdom because of their lukewarmness.

The goal has never been to build a mega-church, but rather to build a mega-strong church. It is no wonder people are waking up and looking for the move of God. Even children will eventually grow bored of a carnival.

For this very reason, some modern Christians find themselves frustrated and unsure of what to do. Just like the saints fleeing apostasy, they may love their church family and even their current pastor, but their allegiance to Christ and the Gospel is creating a hunger for more than what the seeker formula is capable of providing. What's a hungry Christian to do? Some of these Christians will eventually come to the conclusion that they must leave their current church in search of a stronger, God-filled church.

If you find yourself half-starved in one of these seeker churches, please hear me carefully: it is not God's will for you to wither on the vine. And you will not be able to change the direction of your church unless you are the leader. It's a peculiar thing: when a person first joins a church, the devil will fight tooth and toenail to keep them from being faithful to that church. But then, if after a season that church begins to turn lukewarm and compromised, the devil will fight tooth and toenail to keep them there. In fact, they'll somehow become even more committed. Why? Because the devil has no problem with Christians drying up on a half-dead vine.

Too often I've heard good Christians stuck in bad churches declare, "I know things aren't exactly biblical or right here, but I don't *feel* like God has *released* us to leave yet." This can be a very dangerous mindset. This sentiment exalts personal "feelings" over the standard of God's Word. If you are hungrier for more of God, go find more of God!

The "I'm Hungry For More Of God" Parachute

When leaving a church in search for more of God, an *honorable explanation* is certainly called for. Be completely honest with your pastor. Don't be ashamed to be hungry for God—it's required of us. Every church is different, and it may be that your newfound hunger has surpassed the pastor's current vision, teaching style, or assignment. You will only be able to grow as far as the pastor's leadership. Be honest. Be humble. And be respectful.

If the only reason for leaving is your hunger for more, the other five recommendations (*give an honorable time notice, train up your replacement, leave a "going away" offering, request public prayer,* and *request a letter of commendation*) should be very easy to complete. Refrain from gossip and slander, and certainly, if you love the pastor and the church family, continue to pray for them. You will continue to see the pastor and the church members in the community, and there is no reason for it to be awkward. Once again, the key is to be honorable as you depart so God can honor you at your new church.

Finally, never apologize for wanting more of God. If there are any apologies owed, it's from lukewarm believers toward God for *not* being hungrier for His presence or His Kingdom.

9
THE "GEOGRAPHICAL MOVE" PARACHUTE

We have now come to the fourth reason why Christians will leave their church. It is, perhaps, the most common reason for church change in the West. Sadly, it can also be one of the least biblical reasons to leave a church. I am speaking of *the geographical move*. Just as most Americans no longer live and die in the same city anymore, very few Christians will live and die at the same church. There are many reasons why our society has become so unbelievably transient; some are good, some are bad, and some are neutral.

Young people grow up and leave the town or city of their childhood and in doing so, change churches. Kids grow up and go off to college and in doing so, change churches. They then graduate college, find a job, and have to change churches again. Career-minded believers get transferred or promoted to other cities and in answering their employer's call, have to change churches. Military servicemen get deployed or reassigned to another base and in doing so, have to change churches.

Tragedies happen. Loved ones die and families are uprooted to be closer to those who remain. Industries die out, leaving people in search of work. Catastrophes destroy cities and livelihoods, uprooting whole communities. City or community politics turn, and families make the decision to flee for something more family-oriented. Regardless, these scenarios play out over and over again every day in America and around the world. These moves will require the wisdom of God to safely navigate them.

Then there's the influence of the American Dream. The American Dream (to say nothing of modern ambition) has fostered a culture that proclaims nothing is more sacred than a person's dream, and anything that gets in the way of its fulfillment is an enemy. Many Christians leave the church God has assigned them to in order to chase their dreams. But what about God's plan for their lives? We must be careful to always recognize and distinguish between personal dreams and the destiny of God. They are rarely, if ever, the same thing. If we are going to finish our race and glorify the God of Heaven, we're going to have to keep the American Dream and personal ambition on the altar of God every day.

Fire By Night, Cloud By Day

Christians are to be led by the Holy Spirit in all major decisions (and even the little ones too!). Paul taught, "as many as are led by the Spirit of God, they are the sons of God."[1] Part of our uniqueness in Christ is not only the ability to be personally led by God's Spirit, but also the requirement that we *must* be led. Jesus Christ promised us that the Holy Spirit would guide us into all truth.[2] The Holy Spirit is the Spirit of wisdom, and He wants to keep us in the center of God's will, but we must follow His lead.

In Exodus, the moment Israel was released by Pharaoh to go and worship God in the wilderness, "the Lord went before them by day in a pillar of a cloud, to lead them in the way; and by night in a pillar of fire, to give them light; to go by day and night."[3] This was how God would lead Israel, not just out of Egypt on that first day, but for the next 40 years. Exodus 13:22 states that God never took this manifestation away from them until

---

[1] Romans 8:14
[2] John 16:13
[3] Exodus 13:21

they entered the Promised Land. Even now, God still wants to lead us in the way, to give us light.

After experiencing this divine leading for nearly 40 years, consider how Deuteronomy 1:33 looks back and summarizes these phenomena (emphasis mine):

> **[God] Who went in the way before you, to search you out a place to pitch your tents in, in fire by night, <u>to shew you by what way ye should go</u>, and in a cloud by day.**

In essence, Israel didn't move until God moved. When God moved, it was because He was going before them to search out a place for them, not just a place to rest, but also the whole route by which to get there. That tells me God is just as interested in my path as He is in my destination.

As long as God was still, Israel was still. When the fire or the cloud moved, Israel packed up their tents and followed the glory wherever it went. These things were written for our admonition, yet it would seem many today move when the glory is standing still and stand still when the glory is moving.

Churches Aren't Franchises

Some Christians seem to subconsciously believe that churches are like their favorite franchise restaurant and that they'll be able to find the exact same kind of church in whatever town their company moves them to. But what if you can't? What if your boss transfers you and your family to a spiritual wasteland? Are you prepared to sacrifice your family's walk with God to please the boss? Are you prepared to lose your kids to the enemy for a ten percent raise? Or do you have the backbone and faith in God to honorably tell your boss, "I'm sorry, sir. I *cannot* make this move. I'm committed to my church," and then let the chips fall where they may? Do you believe that if God provided that job for you, He is more than able to provide another one?

In the late 1980s, my father, a young, successful, and ambitious mechanical engineer was offered the opportunity to move our family from Tennessee to the Pacific Northwest to manage a massive design-build project. I remember my father taking his time in making the decision and even asking me what I thought about moving across the country, but I'm also sure the career promotion and the financial incentive helped sweeten the deal.

So, at the age of 13, we moved from the Bible-belt South to the environmental extremism of the Northwest. We were faithful Southern Baptists, so the assumption was that we'd just find another Southern Baptist Church once we moved to our new city. I think we believed churches were franchised, and we'd be able to easily find out West what we had left in Tennessee. Alas, it simply was not so. At the time, there was only one Southern Baptist Church in the whole region and as my father recalls, it just wasn't the right fit. My parents ended up settling us into a Covenant Church which, for the uninformed, is like an evangelical Lutheran church.

Ironically enough, after four years in the Pacific Northwest, the completion of the massive engineering project and my high school years, my parents moved back to Tennessee to the exact same community we had left. In fact, they moved right back to the same Southern Baptist Church they missed. They have now served that same church since 1982, minus the four years we spent out West. They learned through experience that churches are not like franchised restaurants. Once you find God's church for you, it is wise to make all of your life's decisions around serving God there.

My Personal Experience With A Driven Boss

When I was a young geologist working for an international engineering firm, my very driven Pakistani boss came to me and asked, "What do you think about moving to Virginia? We have a bid in on a huge highways project, and I'm going to need you to manage it." At that time, I wasn't just deeply committed to my local church, I was also the youth leader. It

GEOGRAPHICAL MOVE

wasn't a paid position, but it was certainly a spiritual assignment from God and my pastor counted on me to disciple the youth in our church. On top of that, it was a deep honor just to be used of God to lead that small group of teenagers.

I didn't even have to pray or "get back" with my boss about my decision. I instantly answered him saying, "Sir, I don't think anything at all about moving to Virginia."

"What do you mean?" he asked.

"I won't be moving to Virginia," I replied.

"Why not?" he asked, a bit put out with me.

"Because everything I have is here in Tennessee." I didn't bother to explain to him my commitment to my local church. We had already had plenty of discussions about Jesus and salvation prior to this, and it didn't seem appropriate to bring it up again at that moment.

He grew more frustrated. "What if I threaten to fire you?"

"Fire me if you have to, sir, but I'm not moving to Virginia," I answered.

He sat in silence for a moment. I meant no disrespect at all. He was a very good boss. Driven and hard, but good. I just wasn't going to abandon my church or my heavenly assignment for an engineering geology assignment.

He finally answered, "You know this will kill your career, right?"

"I realize this won't help it much but I'm not moving," was my answer and it flustered him. It may have been that he never managed someone he could not command, order, or relocate at his whim.

Needless to say, I was greatly stressed by this meeting afterward. I was certain I would be fired, and as mercurial as my boss was prone to be, I didn't know when I might receive the termination notice. My mind began to think of all the other engineering firms where I had connections and who might possibly hire me. Eventually the peace of God came upon me, and I never contacted any other firm. The termination notice never came. In fact, the firm never got the contract to do that engineering work in Virginia. The project simply never materialized. When I look back now, nearly 20 years later, I shudder to think where I might be today if I had failed that mammon test.

Boasting Or Sacrificing

Usually, when it comes to scenarios involving geographical moves, the church member isn't mad at their current church, its message, or even its leadership. Rather, the demands of modern life or even ambition have called or demanded a relocation, and therefore they must move on. In short, these believers are changing churches due to a geographical move dictated by their career or personal ambition. These precious saints need prayer for God's wisdom, favor, and direction. I want to be perfectly clear: it is incredibly dangerous to leave an established church outside of the will of God.

James 4 warns us to take heed, lest we boldly declare "today or tomorrow I will move to such a city, abide there a year, buy, sell, and get gain." What we ought to say is, "If the Lord wills, then I will follow through with *my* plans." James 4:16 warns that such career boastings are prideful and evil. This passage can be directly applied to the modern Christian's career-driven mindset of moving to pursue mammon and please pharaoh. If your geographical move is about money first and God second, then you're chasing money and not God. How do you think this will end for you?

It can easily be argued that whomever or whatever we sacrifice for is our god. Many Christians think it's biblically acceptable to leave a perfectly good church and move across country for a job. I find it ironic, however, that it rarely seems to cross their minds to maybe leave a perfectly good job in order to move across the country to help build a church. Why is changing churches to serve mammon praised, but leaving pharaoh and his brick manufacturing business to build the Kingdom frowned upon?

The "Geographical Move" Parachute

So what's the parachute? How do you safely land in this situation? Pray, pray, pray. In watching Christians make major life decisions, I have wondered how often the glory of God was being followed and how often the

GEOGRAPHICAL MOVE

glory of God was being ignored. Christians must be careful to always include God in their decision-making process and never make a move outside of God's will.

The key to landing safely in this type of transition is to make sure you have sought *and* found the will of God. Seek God to see if the cross-country move is even His will. I would encourage any Christian facing a work-related geographical move to meet with their pastor and ask for wisdom and prayer. Not every promotion or opportunity is from God. Remember, satan is still the god of this world, and as such he has supernatural power to open and close doors, arrange situations and scenarios, tempt and entice, and ultimately mislead and destroy. He would love to get an entire family, or even just a single believer, out of the will of God in pursuit of "the American Dream."

If you move your family outside of the will of God, you'll raise your kids in a place they were never ordained to be raised. If you raise your kids in a place they were never ordained to be, they'll meet people they were never intended to meet. If they meet people they were never intended to meet, they risk falling in love with and marrying someone they were never ordained by God to marry. Only eternity will reveal the damage this kind of event will have done to your lineage and their destinies.

Don't forget that God supplies our needs, not the boss man. God opens up His hand and satisfies the needs of every living thing.[4] James 4:13-16 is very clear: to move to another city without God's permission or endorsement is sin. I personally believe every career-driven Christian will have to pass this test as part of their Christian development.

Concerning military servicemembers: you've got to first make sure God Almighty has called you into the military. Military service is a genuine calling of God, but not everyone in the military was called to be there. Romans 13:1-7 confirms to us that sword-bearing leaders (that's police, security, and military) are God-ordained ministers, executing justice and vengeance. Just make sure that your military service has been ordained by

---

[4] Psalm 145:16

God, and then any deployment or change of station can be trusted to be in God's hands.

Other Christians seem to move upon retirement. I'm not quite sure why a Christian would want to change churches upon retiring in order to find "a better place to live." Wherever God has called you to serve *is* the best place for you to live. If God has called and planted you in a local church, turning 65 or 70 and retiring from the factory has absolutely zero bearing on the church He originally assigned you to. What does retirement have to do with the assignment of God? If you were called to a church before your retirement, guess what? You're still called to serve there after your retirement.

A retirement notice doesn't change the plan of God. If anything, pastors should be able to put a greater demand on their retirees than almost any other demographic in their church. Retirees have more time on their hands to help serve the House of God and build the Kingdom. Their pension or investment funds basically pay them to help in the ministry. One can only spend so much time gardening, sewing, knitting, cleaning the garage, or watching TV. If the secular retiree can volunteer at the local animal rescue, why don't more Christian retirees help their pastor build the Kingdom?

Furthermore, let's be honest. If you're a retiree, you're a lot closer to seeing God face to face than the young married couple just starting a family. I'd strongly encourage you to get to serving in a local church and earn some rewards in Heaven lest you arrive there empty-handed.

A Brief Review

Below are four critical steps to take when you are walking out a geographical move. These are almost identical to the parachute for divine reassignment in Chapter 6.

1. Pray, pray, pray.
2. Submit your plans to leadership and seek their wisdom.
3. Take your time and proceed with caution.
4. Be willing to reverse course if proven wrong.

GEOGRAPHICAL MOVE

Take heart! God wants to get you where He wants you more than you do. He will order your footsteps.

Are you prepared to be fired or demoted in order to stay faithful to the church Jesus Christ assigned you to? Do you fear God or pharaoh? Do you follow the glory of God or the gold of Egypt? Be encouraged, as it has been said many times, "Where God guides, He provides."

10

THE "SEARCH FOR AN EASIER CHURCH" PARACHUTE

The fifth reason for so much intra-church movement is *the search for an easier church*. Let us be very clear: this is one of the most unbiblical reasons to ever change churches. It honestly could be classified as near Christ-denial. Richard C. Halverson is quoted as saying, "Comfortable conformity to the world in which we live today may be the most subtle form of Christ-denial." Searching for an easier church is just such a comfortable conformity. We must never forget that the true calling of Jesus Christ is an upward calling.[1]

Easy is a relative term. Really, the easy church is just the church that has a lower standard than the one you just left. It may seem like the grass is greener at another church, but that may be because there's more manure over there, or maybe it's because you haven't been over there to muck it up yet. Either way, green grass still needs to be cut and that means work— a common allergy of Christians in search of an easier church.

---

[1] Philippians 3:14 NASB

SEARCH FOR AN EASIER CHURCH

It should be obvious to most readers that modern Christians aren't as strong or as mature in their faith as the saints of yesteryear. Rather than finding a church that will disciple and train them into maturity, some saints choose to give in to their sin nature and find an easier church. This is a fulfillment of another end times prophecy. Just as Paul foretold, many believers today can no longer endure sound doctrine, "but after their own lusts shall they heap to themselves teachers, having itching ears; and they shall turn away their ears from the truth, and shall be turned unto fables."[2]

When Paul prophesied that Christians would no longer "endure" sound doctrine, he revealed that sound doctrine places a burden on the hearer—a burden some Christians refuse to bear. Truly, sound doctrine does produce the demand of an upward call upon the life of the believer. This can produce a pressure and discomfort that carnal Christians usually outright refuse.

So what does a carnal Christian do to escape the pressure? They find a pastor that will "take it easy" on them. They seek out and find a preacher that will scratch their itch. They find a pastor who is "always just so encouraging." This attitude propels carnal believers to leave solid Bible churches in search of the easier option. Please hear me: there will always be an easier church! But that doesn't mean you should seek it out. I have personally determined that my church will never be the "easy church." Someone has to be the unswervingly committed church in town—I have determined it's going to be mine (can you imagine if every pastor in every town had the same mindset?).

If you're a Christian, have you sought out the hardcore church in your town, or have you settled into an easier option? If you've not sought out the die-hard church, why not? Is Jesus not worth it to you? Don't you want to be a devoted disciple of Jesus Christ? What do you think your other options are? Do you think Jesus is pleased with half-committed, weak, nominal Christianity? Or mediocre Christianity? Are you not thankful for your salvation? What's your excuse? Why would any Christian settle for less?

---

[2] See 2 Timothy 4:3-4.

Paul's prophecy also indicates that there will be heaps, literally piles and piles, of easy preachers available to scratch any itch imaginable—all in the name of Jesus. That may have been unimaginable in the days of the early Church, but not today. Today, easy churches are the norm, not the exception.

A Church For Everyone

One explanation for the increase in easy preachers can be found in America's love of marketing. It has been observed that when the Greeks got the Gospel, they made a *philosophy* out of it. When the Romans got the Gospel, they made a *government* out of it. When the Europeans got the Gospel, they made a *culture* out of it. And when the Americans got the Gospel, they made an *industry* out of it—and they've been marketing it ever since. These statements are really just another way of recognizing that cultures are usually more effective at perverting the Gospel than Christians are at redeeming their surrounding culture.

The American Church's embracement of marketing strategies has helped to ensure that the carnal saint will always be able to find an easier church. This began in earnest in the late 1970s and early 1980s when certain evangelical church leaders began to purposely take on the marketing philosophies and capitalistic models of the American culture. This mixing of the sacred with the secular was unofficially dubbed by some as "the market-driven church." This was the beginning of the Church adopting the secular attitude of fighting for market share.

Rather than focusing on preaching the Gospel and seeking God for His wisdom, market-driven pastors consulted with business leaders, their books, and the world's wisdom in order to "grow" the church. Forgetting the promise of Jesus Christ—that *He* would *build* His church[3]—active, market-driven pastors learned how to cater to the "non-customer" (a.k.a.—the non-church attender). These pastors began to custom tailor a church "experience" that pleased those not really interested in church. But why

---

[3] Matthew 16:18

would a pastor cater to carnal people and not call them to repentance instead? Because according to the secular marketing experts, "the customer is always right"—and apparently for churches, even the non-customer is right, so pastors should listen to them and give them what they want. After all, we're called to "reach them," right?

To learn what it takes to get a non-customer into church, all you have to do is ask them. Then, since the customer, or in this case the potential customer (a.k.a. the non-church attender), is always right, give it to them and they will come a'running (or so the secular wisdom proclaims). This popular modern church practice should both grieve and terrify us. It should grieve us because it means some of the biggest churches in the land have been built without God's help. It should terrify us because it means there are churches out there that have been grown by catering to man's lukewarm carnality. In essence, these types of churches have adjusted how they "do church" to accommodate the spiritual mediocrity of the non-customer. When these tactics boosted attendance, they erroneously called it the move of God.

So, what does the non-customer want? Well, they maybe kinda want Christ . . . but only if there's no personal cross associated with Him. As a surprise to no one, non-customers avoid church because they don't like the demands associated with God's House, e.g., honor, holiness, conviction, worship, tithing, repentance, etc. What else do they want? Again, as a surprise to no one who walks with God, non-church attenders prefer casualness instead of honor. They want comfort, not holiness. They appreciate motivation but not conviction. And they prefer selfish entertainment in place of holy worship directed toward God Almighty. They want to tip God when they choose to, not give Him their firstfruits. Many prefer not to hear about money at all. Oh, and many prefer personal praise over a call to true repentance.

As it turns out, if you offer this recipe of sorts (no demand, no honor, no holiness, no conviction, no call to repentance, and no call to sacrifice), you can draw the non-customer to your church. In fact, you can draw a LOT of non-customers. They will be converted from non-customer to new customer because you are offering them what they wanted: compromise, convenience, and comfort.[4] The only problem is, the second you stop offering these options, the newly found customers will revert right back to being non-customers, and the pastor is back to square one: just him, his calling to preach, and a Savior waiting to be called upon for help.

This highly effective church-growth strategy has inadvertently, but successfully, produced a full spectrum of churches ranging from ice-cold to lukewarm. One thing it has yet to produce is a hot, on-fire-for-God church. It can't and it never will because it is impossible to build a hot church without the presence of the Holy Spirit and the preaching of the full counsel of God's Word. Sure, the lukewarm church might help a few ice-cold Christians grow a little warmer, but it can also help hot Christians cool off. It's church without the fullness of God. It's a church built on a reduced standard, designed to cater to those whom the very presence of God Almighty couldn't draw. And if God isn't drawing them, then are they really being converted?

The new field of churches ranges from hardcore, doctrine-espousing, holiness-preaching, Holy Ghost-filled churches at one end of the spectrum all the way to the beer-drinking, nightclub-vibed megaplex at the other end—and everything in between. Why so many diverse choices? Why do we find ourselves with more church options than at any time in Church history? Because this is what a healthy, capitalistic market-driven environment can't help but produce. Remember, this is the Gospel according to Peter Drucker.[5] With so many choices available to the "consumer" . . . er . . . I mean carnal Christian, any dissatisfied church member can easily find another church more closely aligned to their opinions, appetites, desires, and carnality. This philosophy produces a church custom-tailored

---

[4] I call this the new godless trinity of Compromise, Convenience, and Comfort.
[5] Peter Drucker (1909-2005) was an agnostic Austrian known for his expertise in systems management and business consultation. He has been referred to as the *Father of Modern Management* and was one of the greatest contributors to the practice of modern business. He purposely taught several influential pastors how to market their church in order to grow it. His secular wisdom is a key component of the seeker-friendly movement.

to please carnal people. It will never tailor a people that can please a holy God.

The market-driven church model has produced the harmful cultural ideology of consumerist Christianity. This is a Christian culture concerned more with what it can consume than what it can contribute. This culture turns Christians into consumers not producers, vagrants not servants, floaters not solid members, dandelions not oak trees, mistresses not covenant partners. These believers are changing churches to stay comfortable, trendy, and catered to. They leave their assigned church in search of an easier church.

The dangerous reality is there will always be an easier church available to the carnal Christian. I'm convinced that in these last days, a carnal believer will be able to keep changing membership from one easy church to the next easier church, backsliding all the way into apostasy and eventually into total Christ-denial—without ever leaving a local church.

The "Easier Church" Parachute

The donning of this parachute begins with self-examination. As a believer you must ask yourself, "Why am I leaving my current church?" What is it about your current church that makes you want to jump ship? Is the pastor too hard? Does he place too much of a demand upon you? Are the sermons too convicting? Are they expecting you to serve somewhere? Are you opposed to taking up your cross—daily? Is the church not cool enough? Not trendy enough? Does the church refuse to endorse your sins?

If you are drawn to easier churches, why? Why do you want less of God? Why do you want less Word? Less church attendance? Less Kingdom responsibility? Less prayer? Less holiness? Less accountability?

Can you not see that these are all symptoms of carnal lukewarmness and apostasy? These desires are symptomatic of an unchecked sin nature, carnal heart, spiritual immaturity, and loss of first love.

Several years ago, an acquaintance of mine told me how he and his family had changed churches in town. He was delighted to share how they were so much happier at their new church, to which I asked why. Why were they so much happier at their new church? He was more than proud to explain that his new church didn't have a Sunday night service, while their previous church did, and according to him, two services on Sunday was too much.

This new church allowed him to have a "family night" with his family, never mind that this could happen on Friday or Saturday night. I wondered, if a family night was really so important to him, why didn't he skip lunches all week and take off half a day on Friday and have their family night on Friday evening? Why does God always have to take the hit? Why can't our money or our career take the hit? Don't we trust God to provide for us? Didn't He declare Himself to be the God who supplies our needs?

My acquaintance led his family away from a solid Bible church and chose their new church based on less responsibility and less service requirements. He chose the easier church. They have since changed churches two more times. Each time has been a step down in spiritual caliber. How will they ever rekindle their first love after so many years of stepping down? Though they are a wonderful couple, they have developed a spiritual lifestyle of retreating into ease.

Leaving any church for the easier church violates New Testament doctrine. The author of Hebrews strictly condemns this sort of mindset (emphasis mine):

> **Now the just shall live by faith: but if any man draw back, my soul shall have no pleasure in him. ³⁹But we are not of them who draw back unto perdition; but of them that believe to the saving of the soul.** **Hebrews 10:38-39**

Choosing the easier church is nothing less than drawing back. And any soul that draws back displeases God. The calling of God is an upward calling. The pursuit of God is an upward pursuit against resistance and opposition. It will never include the pursuit of the path of least resistance. Consider what the Apostle Paul said:

> **Brethren, I count not myself to have apprehended: but this one thing I do, forgetting those things which are behind, and <u>reaching forth</u> unto those things which are before, ¹⁴I <u>press toward</u> the mark for the prize of the <u>high [upward] calling</u> of God in Christ Jesus.**   **Philippians 3:13-14**

Here, the words of the venerable Apostle Paul who, though he had accomplished so much for God at the time of this epistle, declared "I reach forth . . . I press toward . . . the upward calling of Christ." There is simply no room and no excuse for drawing back from God in order to seek out the easier church. To do so requires us to reject the upward calling of God.

In conclusion, spiritually speaking, I don't believe there's any safe way to land at the easy church. Sure, things may go well in the natural for a season, but the seeds of compromise will have been sown and eventually a harvest must come. And only God knows what that harvest could look like. Landing at the easier church is practically abandoning the good fight of faith and retreating in the face of last days' combat. Don't do it!

Some Hard Questions

Below are some serious questions to ask yourself if you're looking for an easier church. After truthfully and humbly answering these questions, you may decide to stay where you are currently planted.

1. Why do you want an easier church?
2. What do you hope to find at an easier church?
3. Are you looking for Christ without a cross?
4. Do you believe you owe God your life?
5. Do you reject God's upward calling?
6. Can you pinpoint when you decided you no longer wanted God's best?
7. What about accountability do you find repulsive?
8. Do you find the commandments of Jesus to be grievous even though He said they are not?

9. How easy is too easy for you?
10. If you keep changing churches for the easier option, do you think you will be able to recognize when you've crossed over into an apostate church? What if you can't?

11

THE "I'M OFFENDED" PARACHUTE

The sixth reason people will leave their church is *offense*. This is absolutely, without a doubt, the most unbiblical reason to ever leave a church. If you've never had the opportunity to get offended at church leadership, just wait, it's coming. This is a test all believers must take *and* pass.

The devil loves to attack believers with the fiery dart of offense. The key is to learn the symptoms of those fiery darts and then quench them with the shield of faith. Very few things can bring a Christian's spiritual momentum to a screeching halt quite like the sin of offense. For that reason, I firmly believe that the enemy keeps tabs on the things that offend us and then uses that knowledge to orchestrate a tactical strike just when we really get going for God.

Offenses often come out of nowhere like a punch to the gut. When this happens, we must arise from the pain and hurt and do the Word of God. We must forgive, go on, and work on the areas of our soul that so easily succumbed to the offense. If we've ever been offended in an area once, we'll probably be attacked and offended in the same area again. Wisdom requires that we take inventory of those weak areas and fortify them with the Word of God. We'll look at how to do this at the end of this chapter.

Getting offended is simply a violation of personal pride. We get offended when we take something too personal. In that regard offenses are good and useful, for they reveal our heart's weaknesses and immaturities. Are offenses real? Absolutely! Jesus declared that offenses are inevitable.[1] They are offered every day, but that doesn't mean we have to receive them. Can they hurt? Sure they can. But Jesus promised that the Holy Spirit would be our Comforter and that He would strengthen us in all of our tribulations, even in the tribulation of offense.

At some point in our Christian development, we'll reach a place where any habitual hyper-sensitivity to offense will be indicative of emotional immaturity. Therefore, we must learn to reject offense and overcome it. But then again, there will always be those who live to get offended. Don't be this person. This is dangerous because to take offense and stay offended is a fruit of the antichrist spirit and a sign of the last days. Jesus taught that rampant offense would be a symptom of the great falling away.

And then shall many be offended, and betray one another, and shall hate one another.   Matthew 24:10

We certainly live in an age when everyone seems to be offended at anything and everything all the time. This verse reveals a sinful three-step process that begins with offense and ends in hatred.

First comes the violation of our personal pride that gives birth to offense. Our offended heart begins to incubate ideas of defensiveness, retaliation, building up walls, or vengeance. These thoughts, if not cast down, will eventually justify the once unthinkable act of betrayal. Betrayal can include anything from harboring a sour attitude and gossip to slander, church abandonment, or even actively working against someone as their adversary. These are behaviors that would have never been considered before the offense took root. No one slanders or abandons someone they love. No one lives to be an adversary against someone they cherish. These actions found their impetus in offense. But offense doesn't stop here.

---

[1] Luke 17:1

If offense and betrayal are left unchecked in our hearts, Jesus promised they would ultimately culminate in hatred. That hatred wasn't there the day before the offense. It wasn't even there the day of the offense. Hatred is slowly grown in the heart of the individual who has been offended and refuses to forgive. Instead of forgiving, they meditate on the offense, rolling it over and over again in their mind, not realizing that every replay of the offense only serves to fertilize hatred. We must not fall into this trap! We must forgive!

Jesus continued in Matthew 24:12 (NASB) to call this entire process lawlessness. The law of God commands us to forgive and drop the charges. To harbor unforgiveness when Jesus commands forgiveness is to practice lawlessness. Jesus revealed in verse 12 that the end result of lawlessness is an ice-cold love. In the original Greek, this verse indicates that practicing lawlessness causes love (*agape*) to become cold (*psycho*), or, the fire of the Godkind of love that was originally in our hearts can grow cold and become frigid. The ultimate agenda of offense is to extinguish the fire of God's love in our hearts. Offense-filled people become hate-filled people.

Offended At Leadership

Offense is the number one way the enemy separates sheep from their shepherd. We must be thoroughly convinced that our pastor is not our enemy. Our enemy—the devil—is our enemy. All of God's people have faced this attack.

Paul addressed this in his epistles. You can hear his heavy heart in Galatians 4:16 when he asked his own disciples, "Am I therefore become your enemy, because I tell you the truth?" Apparently, the Galatian believers got offended over truth delivered by Paul, and as a result, they withdrew from their apostle. They didn't always find Paul offensive. What changed? What could have caused them to turn their hearts against the one man that had done more for them than anyone else? Somewhere a violation of personal pride had crept in and offense was turning them against one of God's mightiest men.

If we want to be mature Christians, we must decide that there is nothing our pastor (or anyone else for that matter) can do to offend us or run us off. My first pastor often observed, "It's amazing that some Christians will quit church over the one thing that offended them, but they won't stick around for the 99 things that have blessed them."

We must learn to believe the best of our fellow church members and to give them the benefit of the doubt. When we understand that God picks our church and we are merely soldiers assigned there by the Lord of Heaven's Armies, it will be a lot easier to handle rough treatment from the drill instructor (or pastor) and the friendly fire of our fellow soldiers.[2]

As Christians, there eventually comes a time when God requires us to grow up past thinking everything is always about us. Reading this chapter may be that moment for you. When we finally learn this Kingdom is not about us, we will begin to extend the same grace we may have often demanded from everyone else. We'll even extend that same grace toward our pastor. If sheep could ever recognize how offensive and off-putting they can be toward their local shepherd, they might learn to extend a bit more grace and mercy toward him.

If you've ever been offended by your pastor, just think about this: there's only one of him you have to deal with, but maybe hundreds of you he has to deal with. If he can look past the offenses of hundreds of sheep and still smile and love you week after week, certainly you can look past his one or two shortcomings and smile back at him, loving him week after week.

Petty Offenses

The following are real complaints heard by real pastors as the complainant departed their church. Have you ever thought or said any of the following?

- *You won't let me take over the church.*
- *You always preach at me.*

---

[2] See Proverbs 27:6.

- *You looked right at me when you said _____.*
- *Your wife didn't say 'hi' to me in the ladies' restroom.*
- *Your wife got a new ring.*
- *Your wife hurt my feelings.*
- *Your wife is involved with Sunday services.*
- *Why does he have to say things that way?*
- *So-and-so looked at me funny.*
- *You didn't pray for that person the right way.*
- *You don't preach from the KJV.*
- *The music is too loud.*
- *The music is too quiet.*
- *There are too many hymns.*
- *The worship is not good enough.*
- *It's too hard here.*
- *You expect too much out of us.*
- *Why can't you be more encouraging?*
- *Too much emphasis on visitors.*
- *Not enough emphasis on visitors.*
- *Too much emphasis on world missions.*
- *Too much emphasis on evangelism.*
- *We're just not being fed here.*
- *I'm not being used here.*
- *There's no love here.*
- *I know I need a pastor; I just don't want it to be you!*

I would strongly recommend that if you happen to find yourself sounding like, relating to, or experiencing any of these complaints, please pause and judge yourself. These are indicators that you may be tracking in a direction that has a 74% failure rate (based on the pastoral poll we saw in the opening of Chapter 5).

The "I'm Offended" Parachute

There is no parachute for the offended parishioner leaving church. The last thing we need to do when we're offended at our church or pastor is to leave. We'll never be able to land safely with bitterness and unforgiveness in us. You don't need a parachute; you need victory. Victory over offense.

Victory over hurt. Victory over unforgiveness. Offense clouds judgment and decision-making ability. Never leave a church because of offense. Offense produces a mental and emotional storm that endangers everything present and future. We must beat offense, not run from it. We must first overcome the offense and then determine if it is God's will for us to change churches. Often it is the heart condition that needs to be changed, not the church.

How To Beat Offense

First, be encouraged. If you're struggling with offense, you're not alone. Offense comes to every one of us. There is no temptation but such as is common to man, and God promises to always provide a way out. God will always provide an exit ramp or two to help us get off the highway of sin. Below are a few escape routes off the highway of offense.

Be honest about the offense. Don't deny that there's a problem. You can't fix a problem you refuse to acknowledge. Be honest with God about it. Talk to Him about it first and foremost. When God told Abram that Sarai would have a child, she mocked with laughter in her heart.[3] This is a form of offense. When the Lord asked her why she laughed, she denied it. The Lord called her a liar. Be honest. Honesty gets help. No honesty, no help.

Ask yourself probing questions. The Bible records many instances when God asked people questions (like the one above). These questions were for their benefit, not God's. He already knew the answer before He asked it. The question was designed to get the person to stop and evaluate their heart. If you ever find yourself offended, ask questions like:

- What am I offended at?
- Why am I offended at this?
- Is there a chance I misheard or misinterpreted this interaction?
- Have I given the offender the benefit of the doubt?

---

[3] See Genesis 18:9-15.

- Have I been offended at this type of interaction before?
- Would a mature Christian find this offensive?
- Would a mature Christian respond as I have?

Immediately pray for the offender. This may be the most important key to overcoming offense. We cannot allow our minds to stew over the violation. We must train ourselves to instantly pray for our offender. We are commanded to walk in love, and nothing instantly manifests the love of God like prayer. Prayer helps us keep our hearts right toward God and toward our offender. If Jesus expects us to pray for our enemies and those that despitefully use us,[4] we can be assured He expects us to pray for our pastor and our church family when they hurt our feelings.

Talk with your offender. Jesus Christ taught us to go to those who have trespassed against us.[5] Clear the air by asking for an explanation or clarification. This will take some humility and courage, but it must be done, especially if it's leadership you are offended at.

I once had one of my elder's wives approach me with great concern. She had walked passed me and another church member having a discussion and heard me say, I'm "disgusted with the elders." Of course she was hurt, but she also knew that to hear such a statement could breed tremendous offense. She quickly came to me, apologized for overhearing a private conversation, but then asked for clarification. She wanted to know what she or her husband, or any of the other elders, might have done for me to be disgusted with them. I had to think for a minute about the statement, if I had said it, and then why I would have said it. It instantly dawned on me that what she had overheard was me saying some outreach we were planning had not been "*discussed* with the elders yet." *Discussed*. Not *disgusted*. Wow! Big difference. What maturity on her part. And the clarity it brought prevented untold calamity.

---

[4] Matthew 5:4
[5] Matthew 18:15

Always do what you can to clear the air and give your offender the opportunity to repent, clarify the issue, qualify their statement, or maybe just reaffirm it.

Determine that your ordained leadership cannot offend you. In John 6:53-67, Jesus taught about eating His flesh and drinking His blood. This was a hard saying and most of His disciples refused to hear it. Jesus asked them point blank, "Doth this offend you?" No one answered His question, but verse 66 states that "many of his disciples went back, and walked no more with him." Can you believe that? The Lord's disciples were offended at Him. Offense caused these disciples to backslide away from Jesus Christ forever. Jesus then turned to the twelve who had not walked away with the others and asked, "Will ye also go away?" Simon Peter answered wisely. His is the answer we all need to resolve in our heart when we find ourselves offended at our God-ordained local church: "To whom shall we go?"

I'm sure Peter no more understood the teaching of eating flesh and drinking blood than anyone else present that day. But he knew enough not to get offended and quit what God was doing in his life. May we all learn to take the same attitude when it comes to staying where God has called us, even in the face of offense and misunderstandings.

Don't let offense separate you from the church or the pastor God has called you to. There's a Kingdom to be built, and God needs you to serve where He has assigned you!

Stay full of the Word. Being full of the Word of God is critical for victory in any area of life. Only the Bible can fill your soul with the strength needed to resist the crushing effects offense can bring.

> **Great peace have they which love thy law, and nothing shall offend them.**   **Psalm 119:165**

What a promise and an endeavor. We can have great peace and never get offended. It is the peace of God that prevents offense. The more peace we have, the less things will offend us. Just because something is offensive doesn't mean we have to be offended at it. Staying full of the Word of God will keep us buoyant in a sea of offense and keep us from abandoning our church the next time our feelings get hurt.

12
CONCLUSION

Jesus Christ has been building His Church for 2,000 years. Generally speaking, almost everything He is doing in the earth, He is doing through the local church. God assigns us, His children, to the church of His choosing, not ours. Every believer is endued with divine graces given by God Almighty to help serve in and build the church where we've been called. Our faithfulness to a local church is critical both for our training and benefit and also for the strength and help we are expected to bring to the other members.

For these reasons, when the time may come to leave one church for another, we must do so with the greatest of care, caution, and honor. Church relocation is not something to be taken lightly or flippantly. We must be careful to make sure our departure neither dishonors Jesus Christ nor harms our church. Much wisdom and prayer are required in such transitional times to ensure a safe landing.

Christians should make every effort to avoid abandoning their post. Unfortunately, this sinful behavior is not just limited to the Western Church experience. When relating his experience of sheep sinfully leaving his church, a dear Zimbabwean pastor related to me: *They just up and leave you and then they judge you from the hole in their parachute.* Please don't do this!

CONCLUSION

History Repeats Itself

History tells us the story of two governors who hated each other. We don't know why they were enemies, only that there was a strong enmity between them. These two governors oversaw bordering territories and answered to the same emperor, so perhaps the tension arose due to competition. Or maybe their animosity was due to their conflicting policies that inadvertently affected their respective domains. Regardless, knowing the pride often found in rulers, there was little hope for the two ever making amends. But oddly enough they did. Not only did they make amends, they actually became friends.

The name of the first governor was Pontius Pilate. He was the governor over the province of Judea. His domain included Jerusalem. The name of the second governor was Herod Antipater (a.k.a. Herod the Tetrarch and King Herod).[1] Part of his domain included Galilee, the area where Jesus was the most active.

So how did these two Roman rulers, who oversaw part of the Roman territory known as Israel and answered to Caesar Tiberius, make amends and become friends? They found a common cause. A common enemy. In their case it was Jesus Christ. "And the same day Pilate and Herod were made friends together: for before they were at enmity between themselves."[2] This philosophy has played out for millennia and has famously been summarized as "the enemy of my enemy is my friend."

"But what in the world does this have to do with leaving church honorably?" you may be asking. It is practically a spiritual law that when people leave their church dishonorably and bitter, they will automatically gravitate towards other embittered former church members. Ironically, these always seem to be people they would have had nothing to do with while they served at the same church. While they were under the same pastor, they were enemies, but once they leave dishonorably, they find common ground. They'll begin running together, fellowshipping together,

---

[1] Herod really wasn't a king so much as he was a ruler over a fourth part (*tetrarch*) of Judea. His domain included Galilee and Perea.
[2] Luke 23:12

even attending a new church together. Like Herod and Pontius Pilate, the former enemies become friends over a new common enemy—their old church. I would not recommend building any friendship upon the foundation of destroying the Body of Christ. That is a friendship birthed in hell.

Social Media "Friends"

Some years ago, we had a lady leave our church with a very bitter and hostile attitude. She left unrepentant of flagrant sin. Before long she took her grievance to that wonderful platform of adult decorum known as social media, even calling me and our church out by name. As a surprise to no one, within a few hours of chumming the internet's waters with slander, her thread was filled with comments—all from former members of our church. Of course, she was still friends with most of our church family, so many of our members got to read the lies, slander, vitriol, and hate. And they got to see all of their former church family hop on the feeding frenzy, running us down, and encouraging "themselves in an evil matter."[3]

This was, of course, very painful for many in our church. Some felt like the psalmist when he lamented in Psalm 41:9, "Yea mine own familiar friend, in whom I trusted, which did eat of my bread, hath lifted up his heel against me." The feeding frenzy of that post lasted for a few days and then, as was predictable of the modern attention span, people moved on to the next topic of interest (probably a cat video).

When I heard the names of all the former church members feeding on the gossip and slander of their fornicating sister in Christ, one thing stuck out: every single one of those people had also left with some sort of sexual sin in their life. It was uncanny. Sexual sin was the one thing they all had in common. That and our church being their enemy.

While they were at our church, most of these people never so much as acknowledged one another. Now that they had left us and were "free," they were like Pontius Pilate and Herod—new best buds. All these years later, there is not a single one of those families better off today than the day they

---

[3] Psalm 64:5

CONCLUSION

left our church. Most of them have suffered the catastrophic consequences of sexual perversion, e.g., divorce, molestation, adultery, premarital sex in their children, etc.

I conclude this book with a word of warning: if you've left a church and now find yourself fellowshipping with other former church members, please judge yourself. According to what you have read in this book, did your new friends leave honorably? Is your fellowship in the light, or do your conversations revolve around "that church"? Do you reminisce and continually rehearse all your hurts and everything "that church" did wrong? Have you and your new "friends" ever stopped to pray for "that church"? Have you ever noticed that "that church" has probably continued on without you, preaching the Gospel, winning the lost, discipling the saints, and serving God?

Was "that church" perfect? No. No church is perfect. But I can guarantee you this, they're busy marching on with Jesus! Won't you?

ACKNOWLEDGMENTS

Once again, special thanks to the editing team of Eva Dingwall, Kiley Baldwin, Hannah Keith, and Dr. Shayla Carew for the countless revisions, editing sessions, and last-minute mark-ups. Thank you to Darrell Kerley for the cover layout and Marlin Peterson for the parachuting sheep design. I also wish to thank all of my proofreaders: Bobbie Scudder, Patti Newman, Danielle Girt, AJ Vaughn, Pastor Brett Scudder, and Casey Dudek. All of your feedback was invaluable. Thank you to Pastor Andy Smith for taking the time to teach me the Lutheran perspective on church membership and departure and to Father Christiano Nunes for the time spent discussing Catholic doctrine concerning church membership. Thank you also to Pastor Phil McMichael, Pastor Darren Osburn, Dr. Michael Jacobs, Mark Nauroth, and Pastor Scott Parkison for their doctrinal critique and feedback. I am especially grateful for my wonderful wife, Manda, for keeping things going as we finished up this book.

Other books by J. Christopher McMichael

Building Sound Doctrine (minibook)

*Samson:
Secrets to Destroying Your Life and Ministry*

*Fat, Broke, & Crazy:
Rediscovering the Fruit of Self-Control*

*Parachutes for Sheep:
The Minibook*

For more information
visit www.EngraftedWord.org